IN SEARCH OF SOUTH AFRICA'S
PERFECT WOMAN

BY KEVIN McCALLUM

Other books by Two Dogs:

293 Things Every SA Man Should Know
My Dad – by South African Sons
I Can Do That! Fitness for the Lazy Guy

Coming soon…

Sports Holidays: Where to Go and When
Women's Bodies: A User's Manual

TWO DOGS
Books men read

Fix the tap. Clean the car. Argue with your boss. Grab a cold beer with friends on the way home from work. Watch the rugby. Put the children to bed. Argue with your bank on the internet. Call the plumber to fix the tap properly. Listen to "I told you so." Polish your shoes. Make up with your girl. Go to bed.

Two Dogs publishes books men read. So join us in getting stuck into the Big Fs – fitness, friendship, fast cars, fashion, food and fornication – plus a whole lot of stuff that leaves the F off.

Two Dogs publishes books you're as likely to be seen with on the beach or in the pub as you are with your feet up at home. Quick reads, long reads, books you can dip into, books you can get your teeth into, pages you can flick through again while you're waiting for her to finish her hair. "Does my bum look big in this?" Shhh! I'm reading. This is Two Dogs.

Some men choose to read alone, others prefer to argue the point with friends. Read them, argue them, even use them to prop up your wobbly table in the lounge when you've finished. Either way, no Two Dogs man will ever say "I don't read books" as if it's a badge of honour.

Grrrr.

Two Dogs is published by SchreiberFord Publications and Struik.
info@twodogs.co.za
www.struik/twodogs.co.za

Published by Two Dogs
an imprint of SchreiberFord Publications and Struik Publishers

•

SchreiberFord Publications
PO Box 50664, The Waterfront, Cape Town, 8001

Struik Publishers
(a division of New Holland Publishing (South Africa) (Pty) Ltd)
PO Box 1144, Cape Town, 8000
New Holland Publishing is a member of Johnnic Communications Ltd

•

First published 2006

1 3 5 7 9 8 6 4 2

•

Publication © 2006 Two Dogs
Text © 2006 Kevin McCallum
Cover image © 2006 Gallo Images/www.gettyimages.com

•

•

Publishing manager: Daniel Ford
Managing creative director: Grant Schreiber
Managing editor: Tim Richman
Cover design: Sean Robertson
Design: Elize Schultz
Production manager: Valerie Kömmer

•

Reproduction by Hirt & Carter Cape (Pty) Ltd
Printed and bound by Paarl Print, Oosterland Street, Paarl, South Africa

•

ISBN 1-920137-04-1

info@twodogs.co.za
www.twodogs.co.za

Little sausage dog looking nervously at the mustard

Contents

About the author:

Kevin McCallum is the chief sports writer for
The Star, *The Saturday Star* and *The Sunday Independent*. He
gets paid to travel the world, drink beer and watch sport.
This is his first book.

*To the perfect women I know, have known
and will one day know.*

INTRODUCTION

Some years ago, I knew a man who told me he drank beer every day, every night and most lunchtimes, not merely because he liked the taste, but because he was a man with a mission. "I have heard," he slurred, "that South African Breweries has made a bad beer. I am trying to find it." We lost touch shortly after that so I'll never know if his quest for the unholy grain was successful. I hope it was.

He did find something else, though, a prize even more precious than beer and rarer than a bad bottled lager. The last time I saw him he was dipping his head towards his beer with the tentative squint of a scientist, the smile of a saint and the audience of a quite delicious-looking woman. I had seen her on the periphery of our group for a while: striking face, naughty eyes and body and, from the little I spoke to her, I recall her voice had a slow gin-and-tonic sashay. One day she sat down on the seat next to my friend's, ordered a drink and the two got to chatting. Their bar stools got closer with every passing day and pretty soon they were a couple, content to spend their best waking hours together in a dreamy haze. He spoke, she listened, she spoke, he listened, they laughed, held hands, gave each other pecks on the cheeks, shared cigarettes and, in an act that signified true love, bought rounds out of that small pile of change that builds up on the bar counter in front of seasoned drinkers. He had found his perfect woman.

Or rather, she had found him, because the only thing he was looking for was a bad beer. (Funny, I never have problems finding a bad beer. It's always the last one of the evening, the one that makes you feel atrocious the next day.) She had identified him as her mate of the species and had made a wonky beeline for him. While they were hardly Mickey Rourke and Faye Dunaway, and their life was hardly *Barfly*, the two of them did make a quite perfect couple, both of them holding down decent enough beers – sorry, jobs – both witty and intelligent and, quite importantly for my friend, she was beautiful, even before he started drinking. She was, to use a marketing term, a complete fit for the product he had to offer. She was the perfect woman for him.

I would be telling a monstrous fib if I were to pretend I wasn't jealous of my bad-beer-seeking friend, because I was and still am outrageously dirty that he discovered his perfect woman simply by sitting still on a bar stool for hours on end and doing what he does best. Even if they are not still together – I think the pub they met in has closed down, so if you see a couple in your local that fits the above description, buy them a drink from me – damn it all, it was the closest thing to an arranged marriage as I have ever seen among grown adults. I'm surprised the barman didn't ask for lobola. Finding a mate isn't supposed to be that easy; or rather, it is, but it isn't. And because it isn't, I have been able to compile an entire book dedicated to the heterosexual man's eternal search for the perfect woman.

"Perfect woman." Those are two words you will hear a lot as you trip along through this book. They are two words that make no sense, because there is no such thing as a perfect woman. I know this because every woman I know has told me so, some with more glee than is necessary when discussing the devils of dating with a bachelor of long and proud standing, as I have been these 30-odd years (yes, that's right girls, still under 40).

"But, what about Bo Derek in *10*?" I whine. "She wasn't too far off perfect. She was beautiful, had bits that bounced in a gold bikini when she ran on the beach in slow-motion, and was well educated."

"Kevin, just because she liked to shag to Bolero does not make her well-educated," sighed one imperfect female friend, but I wasn't listening by then. In fact, I've just made up her retort, right now. I was lost in that scene where Derek runs naked to fix a stuck record player while gagging to boff a confused Dudley Moore. Why, oh why did he turn her down when she said she wanted to "do him a favour"? And why, oh why, did he wear a full cotton tracksuit on a Mexican beach?

I offer other potentially perfect women to imperfect women for appraisal:

Famke Janssen?
"Could you call out her name during sex?"

Carla Gugino?
"Who?"
(She's the mommy in *Spy Kids*, thank you very much, and hey, she does it for me.)

Angelina Jolie?
"Well, besides the whole Brad Pitt thing, she's a skank. Also, she has too many tattoos. And she married an ugly old guy and she carries vials of blood around. You know, she's such a bad judge of men, she likes girls as well and she'd only be using you for sex and that's the last thing you want, isn't it?"
Er, yes, that's right. I wouldn't want anyone just to use me for sex, particularly anyone who might bring her girlfriend with.

How about Jennifer Aniston?
"Too nice and she's Greek. You know how much trouble you'll get into if you mess her around. And her hair's too nice. You'll mess it up. And as for the whole Brad Pitt thing… "

Paris Hilton? This was a double bluff. I think she's heinous, but for the sake of the experiment, I wanted the female perspective.

"I've seen bigger tits in a bird bath. And she's just a rich skank."

Ah, a better class of skank, fair enough.

Cameron Diaz?

"Her mouth's too big, she laughs too much and she sleeps with young boys. I mean, she's like totally too old for Justin."

Brittany Murphy?

"Skank."

Yeah, but skank can be good, can't it?

What about Jessica Alba?

"Can't act and she snogged Bruce Willis."

Sharleen Spiteri?

"She's Scottish."

So, that's one thing cleared up. Just as there is no such thing as the quintessential Mr Right, there is no such thing as an utterly perfect woman – not even celebrities! I must confess that deep down inside I have known this for some time, but as one who always looks for the good side of people and believes that one woman's imperfections are the next man's perfections (particularly if that man is a plastic surgeon), I believe that there is a perfect woman out there for me. Mind you, there was also that one time I believed I could fly, but that's not a story you want to hear and not one I am allowed to repeat, although I so nearly did fly, I swear (I even tried to forget to hit the ground, just as Douglas Adams wrote, the lying sod). But I have faith that one day I shall happen upon a good soul with whom I'll be able to lovingly split that large pile of change on the bar counter without so much as the smallest bitch about the fact that her gin and tonics cost more than my lagers. My perfect woman is out there, I tell you.

My faith that Miss (or, in the case of Bo Derek, Missus) Perfect is out there waiting for me is still strong because of the encounters I have had with women who have had elements of what I am looking for, though this faith of mine has been sorely tested over the 30-odd years of my life (there it is again, ladies: under 40! Act now! Contact the publisher for my telephone number and other vital statistics before I head off into middle age). These encounters, some of them of the third-base kind, have all been special in their own particular and peculiar ways, some more peculiar than I would have liked, and the particulars of others will remain under wraps lest the women in question buy this book and run screaming to their lawyers that I have done them a disservice by mentioning our mutual servicing.

But I am a gentleman and have resolved that throughout this book I will change the names of people involved in various situations to protect the innocent and, more importantly, the guilty. To all the girls I have loved or even vaguely met before, who've staggered in and out my door – yes, all of you – your secrets are safe with me. However, should someone guess your name and tell you, then I wish to state here and now that I distance myself from those clever clogs and wish to inform you that all royalties of this book have been locked up in a trusty fund should you think about taking me to court.

For this is not a kiss-and-tell book so beloved of retired rugby players; this is an educational tome for modern single men. This is for men who dream of finding the perfect woman, but don't know where to look, and don't even know what parts a perfect woman should be made up of. I have sent out search parties to the far ends of the Earth, as well as to Boksburg, in the making of this book. Pubs have been frequented, clubs have been lounged in, gyms sweated in and supermarkets loitered in. No rock has been left unturned and no, she is not to be found under a rock. I have seen men sacrifice themselves selflessly in the making of this book, surrendering their hearts to imperfect women who have suckered them in with a façade of flawlessness under cover of darkness only for the cracks to start showing at first light when it was too late to run. That such deviousness exists in the world still brings a chill to my bones. Some of those loyal lads escaped to search again, but the others... their names will be engraved on the wall of remembrance that will be erected with all the profits made from this undertaking.

This is not, however, merely a book for men looking to get involved in a relationship or even, heaven forbid, married. *In Search of South Africa's Perfect Woman* is also a reference book, both for those wishing to jump into a gene pool for a quick dip, put in a Roland Schoeman-like 50 metres before heading off for a splash somewhere else, and those who would like to know just how warm the water is before getting in. That said, it is also a work that non-single men should read, just so they know what hell the world of dating and singledom has become and, at times, how lucky they are to be out of it. Hell, it's a book for their wives and girlfriends, as well. Measure yourself up against the perfect woman; do not fear if you fall short, it is nothing to be ashamed of. Perfection is, er, perfect, and very few of us are perfect.

However, if you are several levels away from the standard that is set in these pages, do try and shape up, there's a good lass.

I am a bachelor of long and proud standing. Many of my best friends are bachelors, even those who are married, and especially those who have just got divorced. It's a state of mind, you see, a way of looking at the world. Bachelorhood is merely a description of freedom that we should all have, a freedom that, for men, is restricted and confused by only one thing – the search for the perfect woman. It's a never-ending topic, an eternal journey that never reaches a conclusion. It's almost as long a search as the quest to find a bad beer.

1

WHAT IS THE PERFECT WOMAN?

Down at Lake Wanaka in Central Otago on New Zealand's South Island, they take their search for the perfect woman very seriously. For those who have not visited New Zealand, it is – as shallow as this may sound – not a country known for the physical beauty of its females. While they may all be stunning on the inside, the outsides leave a lot to be desired. And I reckon a girl has to have at least the smallest smidgin of skin-deep beauty.

During a trip to Dunedin recently, I spotted three good-looking girls: two of them were Australian and the other was from South Africa. As for the rest, and being kind, they were on the wrong side of plain, not much to look at. But they were very friendly – a little too friendly, actually. A South African lady seated next to me on the flight to Auckland from Perth had warned me that New Zealand women are very forward and that, if I wasn't careful, I might just find myself being chatted up by one in a bar and carted off to some dark corner for some dark goings on. She grabbed me by the arm and looked me in the eyes with a worried expression: "They're desperate, I tell you. You're an attractive young man, they'll hunt you down. Be careful. You don't know how desperate they are. All they want to do is to get you into bed with them."

I had a quiet chuckle to myself and, at first, I looked forward to being chatted up by a Kiwi Kickie-wickie – nothing wrong with being propositioned when you are a single guy in town to watch the rugby – but a quick inspection of the female side of the population on the flight from Auckland to Dunedin soon put me right. The stories were all true. This was a nation of ten-beer handicap women, a country of girls with "nice personalities", who were beautiful on the inside because they certainly weren't much cop on the outside. It explained two important things about New Zealand: firstly, why it has a population of only four million people and, secondly, why the men drink so much.

Now I know that New Zealand once had a Miss Universe – back in 1983 if I know my pageants – but that was almost an entire generation and several million beers ago. She was married to Murray Mexted, the All Black eighth man, who has admitted that he finds South African women amongst the most beautiful in the world. Perfection in Kiwi women, therefore, has had to be judged on other, more robust attributes, and the good people down at the Bullock Bar at Lake Wanaka have been running a "Perfect Woman" competition for the last couple of years over their Labour Weekend at the end of October. Owner of the Bullock Bar, Stu Bart, offers $1,000 as first prize, plus a day in a corporate box at Eden Park, for the woman who lives up to the ideals of the perfect southern woman.

The list of tasks set the entrants includes:

Guy bucking (yes, that's right, bucking)

Clearing ten balls from a pool table – or as many as possible in three minutes

Fitting a set of snow chains

Banging in a four-inch nail (Obviously Kiwi men aren't all that well endowed…)

Opening a quart of Speight's Gold Medal Ale without using a bottle opener

Shooting

Digging in a fence post

Jetboat sprinting on Lake Wanaka

Backing a trailer loaded with hay, stacking and unstacking it

Tipping over a ram

Darts

Blowing a dog whistle

Singing "The Southern Man Song"

It has become a popular competition, with 50 women entered by pubs from across New Zealand. The winners are usually in their early twenties, strong girls of stout farming stock from the hard South. The 2003 winner was 24-year-old Jodie Ruddenklau, a shepherd from Omarama. "Apart from being perfect, Jodie is also a whiz at throwing a fleece and a sharp shooter!" exclaimed the bar's website. The 2002 winner was 23-year-old Kate Cameron, "daughter of Walter the perfect man and Sandy, who has made him perfect. Kate was brought up on a sheep and beef property in the Waitaki Valley and studied Viticulture, Wine and Food in Christchurch, before working with Gibbston Valley wines as a block manager for two years. She now works at the Wanaka Bullock Bar and also organises the Perfect Woman competition."

Talented, indeed, but it brings into sharp relief the need to have some form of definition for the perfect woman. Hearty farming stock might be just the thing for lonely men on the South Island, but a woman who can open a beer bottle with a spatula and a quick wrist may be a bit of a liability at a black-tie function in London. Similarly, an "It" girl from London wouldn't be much good if you needed a ram tipped over, a fence post dug or a fleece tossed. It would be right daft to go on a quest without having an idea of just what we are looking for. Because we are all of us of a different bent, the definitions will allow for some push and pull for those of you with more exotic tastes.

As she has managed to survive the hair flicks of Bryan Ferry and the indiscretions of Mick Jagger, supermodel and actress Jerry Hall is as qualified as any to kick off the broad description of the perfect woman with her famous quote: "My mother said it was simple to keep a man: you must be a maid in the living room, a cook in the kitchen and a whore in the bedroom. I said I'd hire the other two and take care of the bedroom bit."

A wise and wholly un-liberated woman was Jerry's mother, who gave birth to a woman who, at 19, became the first true supermodel, a tall Texan cowgirl so beautiful that the writer Cosmo Landesman described her as having "glamour that made grown men go weak at the groin". I think I speak for most modern men when I say that they do not need the first two attributes either and would be more than happy to employ two others to do the cooking and the cleaning, but hiring someone to keep you happy in the bedroom is still frowned upon. Miss Hall, for whom Ferry wrote *Cry, Cry, Cry* after she left him for Jagger, has never elaborated on just what keeping a man happy in the bedroom consists of, purring that if she told us "it wouldn't be private, would it?" And so we are left to wonder just what Jagger was missing out on when he was out gallivanting around town. She isn't totally perfect, though, admitting that she has big feet, has no problem with women with big noses and small breasts (she thinks that people are too obsessed with looks) and finds Henry Kissinger the most "stimulating" man she has ever met.

So, a good start by Miss Hall, but a flawed one. Others have volunteered their definition of the perfect woman to me. Two female friends said that there was no such thing as a perfect woman or a perfect man, although they did place rather more emphasis on the latter than the former. They haven't had the best of times with men, those two. Another friend called me to say that the perfect woman was three foot tall with a flat head and wore roller skates. "So you can put your empty beer bottle on her head and push her to the fridge to get another one," he giggled softly over the phone in case his wife heard. He also made a reference to this version of the perfect woman having retractable teeth so that she… no, I will not sully this book by repeating the rest of his description. For, indeed, I am a sensitive modern man (in between drinks) and the search for the perfect woman is not one that should be demeaned by schoolboy jokes. I did find a joke that tickled my fancy, though:

An extraordinarily handsome man decided he had the God-given responsibility to marry the perfect woman so they could produce children beyond comparison.

With that as his mission he began searching for the perfect woman.

After some time on his quest, he met a farmer who had three stunning, gorgeous daughters, who positively took his breath away. So he explained his mission to the farmer, asking for permission to marry one of them.

The farmer simply replied: "They're all looking to get married, so you came to the right place. Look them over and select the one you want." So the man took the first daughter on a date.

The next day the farmer asked for his opinion.

"Well," said the man, "she's just a weeeeee bit, not that you can hardly notice, but pigeon-toed."

The farmer nodded and suggested the man date one of the other girls; so the man went out with the second daughter.

The next day, the farmer again asked how things went.

"Well," the man replied, "she's just a weeeeee bit, not that you can hardly tell, cross-eyed."

The farmer nodded and suggested he date the third girl to see if things might be better. So he did.

The next morning the man rushed in exclaiming: "She's perfect, just perfect! She's the one I want to marry!" So they were wed right away.

Nine months later the baby was born. When the man visited the nursery he was horrified: the baby was the ugliest, most pathetic-looking human you can imagine. He rushed to his father-in-law asking how such a thing could happen considering the parents.

"Well," explained the farmer, "she was just a weeeeee bit, not that you could hardly tell, pregnant when you met her."

Poets have written heaps on women and their love of them, comparing them to summer days, various flowers and angels in the heavens above. Byron told us how a woman walked in beauty, Shakespeare got all silly over the darling buds of May, Tennyson gave us "Marriage Morning", Yeats had a rose growing in his heart and who can forget (if not pronounce) Burns's "A Red, Red Rose"? (*O my luve's like a red, red rose,/ That's newly sprung in June;/ O my luve's like a melodie,/ that's sweetly play'd in tune...*).

Climate, vegetation and winged ethereal beings are all fine and dandy, but few of them have reached the heights of William Wordsworth's appropriately titled "Perfect Woman", written about his wife, Mary:

She was a phantom of delight
When first she gleam'd upon my sight;
A lovely apparition, sent
To be a moment's ornament;
Her eyes as stars of twilight fair;
Like twilight's, too, her dusky hair;

But all things else about her drawn
From May-time and the cheerful dawn;
A dancing shape, an image gay,
To haunt, to startle, and waylay.

I saw her upon nearer view,
A Spirit, yet a Woman too!
Her household motions light and free,
And steps of virgin liberty;
A countenance in which did meet
Sweet records, promises as sweet;
A creature not too bright or good
For human nature's daily food;
For transient sorrows, simple wiles,
Praise, blame, love, kisses, tears, and smiles.

And now I see with eye serene
The very pulse of the machine;
A being breathing thoughtful breath,
A traveller between life and death;
The reason firm, the temperate will,
Endurance, foresight, strength, and skill;
A perfect Woman, nobly plann'd,
To warn, to comfort, and command;
And yet a Spirit still, and bright
With something of angelic light.

You have to wonder, though, whether Wordsworth was afraid of his missus. First he calls her a phantom, then a spirit, a traveller between life and death, and then he tells us that she haunts him, before startling him and then waylaying him. Unless, of course, " waylay" was 18th-century slang for getting laid. You think I jest? Look at the second verse – all that talk about "steps of virgin liberty", "countenance" and "praise, blame, love, kisses, tears and smiles" – the man is obviously talking about hanky panky. He was the Snoop Dogg of his day was Wordsworth, except that he was not quite as direct about the manner in which he would be getting down with his ho, and whether Missus Wordsworth got a good sorting out in the back of the horse cart is not public knowledge.

To be honest, poetry is a large part of why so many of us are looking for the perfect woman. The immortalisation of the female of the species in such luscious terms is probably why we search for a female with the softest skin, the silkiest hair, the most musical of voices, complementary of minds and perfectly sculpted of bodies. In one of the best known stories of a man searching for the perfect woman, a Greek fella called Pygmalion, the King of Cyprus, felt that the women he came into daily contact with were bad news and decided he would never marry. Being a decent sculptor when he wasn't being a king, he fashioned for himself his perfect woman from, so the story goes, ivory. It was so beautiful and so lifelike that Pygmalion fell in love with his creation – and turned a little weird. He would caress it and buy it presents, he put rings on its fingers, bought it a dress and draped pearls across its breasts. He began calling it his wife and would, according to some texts, lay down next to it on his couch. She was the perfect woman for him.

But, perhaps bothered by the whispers of the next-door neighbours and the fact that his bird was frigid in the sack, Pygmalion wanted something more flesh and blood than carved white bone. At the festival of Aphrodite, the multi-tasking goddess of love, beauty and sexual rapture, Pyggy offered a prayer that was to be echoed by all seekers of perfect woman: "You gods, who can do all things, give me, I pray you, for my wife one like my ivory virgin."

Now Aphrodite was something of a flighty chick, a woman who was created when the chief of all the gods, Uranus, was castrated by Cronus, who was his son. Cronus tossed his old man's meat and two veg into the sea, which set the sea off, and it frothed and bubbled as though he had thrown dry ice into it. From the resulting foam, called "aphros" in Greek, Aphrodite came into being and first set foot on land in Cythera. (She is also sometimes called Cythera, and would be mightily annoyed to find out that there is a porn star using her name. My friend tells me that Cythera the porn queen can perform tricks that would turn on Uranus – even a castrated Uranus.) As the word aphrodisiac comes from Aphrodite, perhaps there is money to be made from bottling sea foam and marketing it as a natural form of Viagra. Before you know it they'll be selling vodka and sea foam shots down at your local. (Just so you know, Homer, the Greek poet and philosopher – not Simpson – described Aphrodite as the daughter of Zeus and Dion, but the sea foam story is much more fun.)

From what we know about Aphrodite, she was married off to one of the more grimy gods, whom she later left. She also set up Paris of Troy with Helen of Sparta, so starting the Trojan War and presenting the world with the unbelievable story of the Trojan Horse, not to mention the movie *Troy*. Plus, she had a magical girdle with which she entranced men and shagged Adonis as well as many other lucky mortals. She was a busy perfect woman, was our Aphrodite.

But where was I? Oh yes, the praying Pygmalion. Anyway, Aphrodite heard his prayer and, after checking out the statue, decided to grant him his wish, as she thought it resembled her. He went home and gave his statue bird a kiss on the lips, only to find that she was warm and pliable. He looked again and found that she had been turned into flesh and bone and other nice soft bits. Her name was Galatea and they lived happily ever after. It is not recorded as to whether Pygmalion was banned from further sculpting by his beloved lest he get bored of her and take a notion to carve himself a bit of something on the side, but their story has struck a chord with seekers of perfect woman all over the world, with a 1,000-pound, eight-foot, $100,000 bronze statue of her erected in St Petersburg, Florida. Salvador Dali, suffering from ill health, went to stay in the Galatea Tower after a fire at the Pubol Castle. He died in the tower in 1989. In business circles, the human resources crowds have come up with the Pygmalion and the Galatea effects, which are all to do with self image and the liking of your self image. If your boss starts sculpting a statue of a perfect woman out of waste paper and then moves it into your office at work, it may be time to seek employment elsewhere, especially if he kisses it in public and offers up prayers to some dodgy Greek goddess.

So what can we learn from all of the above? Well, that the search for a perfect woman is no walk in the park for a start and that the Greeks have one up on the rest of us when it comes to finding Miss Right. But not all of us can use the "if you build her she will come" approach to appropriating a partner. We know what we want, but we don't know how to get it. You can't just knock together a perfect woman with some ivory, a chisel and a fevered imagination, nor can you buy the perfect woman from an adult shop and blow her up. Although, on the perfectwomen.com website, a cosmetic site, they do offer breast enlargement cream.

The Chinese believe that a perfect woman must be tender because she "knows well that her tenderness is greater than the firmness of an angry fist, which can usually be beaten by a delicate beautiful finger. The perfect woman must often have tears in eyes. Tears are a woman's perfume, intelligence and sexiness. Where there is the life hope, there must be the woman's tears. Tears are the special kind of warning and reminder for the man. The perfect woman should show her love in the candle light."

Despite the hopeful belief we all carry that we are all unique, we all have traits that put us into stereotyped boxes from which the perfect man will be able to identify and, if he's lucky, pluck his perfect woman. There is no one perfect woman, my friends; she wears disguises aplenty and has many shields. Uncovering those disguises and knocking back the shields, now that's the trick.

WHAT DO MEN WANT FROM WOMEN?

Sex. As Hunter S Thompson said, "That is all ye know and all ye need to know."

WHAT DO WOMEN WANT FROM MEN?

"Despite my thirty years of research into the feminine soul,
I have not been able to answer… the great question that has
never been answered: what does a woman want?"
– Sigmund Freud

He really should have known, old Siggy. Women want
sex, but with a twist, which may, for some of you
unreconstructed men out there, seem as silly as beer with
a lemon stuck in the neck. At the base of things, we all
want sex. It's what drives us as human beings, from Adam
and that sea foam-laced apple he had forced upon him by
Eve, to the strait-laced spinster who mans the telephone
reception at your office. Women want sex, except that they
don't refer to it as sex and will refer to it as sex only after
the two of you start having problems in your relationship.
Men, as with their penises, have several phrases for sex, none
of them particularly original: a good seeing to, doing the
dirty, making the beast with two backs, shagging, giving her
one, knocking boots, bumping uglies, doing the wild thang,
having it away, getting jiggy with it, humping, banging,
boning, bonking, boffing, etc. This stems from our teenage
days when inventing names for sex and sexual organs was
considered a legitimate means of entertainment during
lunch break in high school. One pal of mine managed
to come up with 46 different names, but then again his
father had been married four times and his collection of
pornographic magazines at home was legendary.

  (As an aside, an American family planning website
encourages parents to be responsible when talking to their

children about sex and to use the correct, clinical expressions for sexual organs. I am thankful that my parents never saw fit to use the words "vulva" and "vagina" in my presence, and left me to call my penis "Junior". Having said that, Billy Connolly thinks that vagina is a much nicer word than scrotum. "Scrotum just sounds ugly," he said. "Now vagina, there's a beautiful word. Imagine if you saw that on the side of a cereal box at breakfast: 'Win a two-week holiday in Vagina!' Wouldn't you want to go there for a visit?" Indeed.)

Using these words in a woman's presence will not get you sex, and while I know some girls who do not flinch at the words "shag", the phrase "fancy a fuck" has about as much chance of succeeding as George Bush does in bringing peace to Iraq. In fact, I think Dubya may have said that very phrase to Saddam Hussein just before he invaded. So try not to use any of your teenage euphemisms for sex, as funny or as honest as you may think they are, around girls. And while the female of the species may like dancing to rap songs, using a line that includes any reference to "bitches" and/or the readiness of your junior, is likely to get you a good shoeing. When you find the perfect woman, she will want you to be a man, or at least to act like one.

But I digress or regress, or both. Know this and know it well: women want sex as much as us, but they are not as driven by things that go bonk in the night as we men are. Sex with the perfect woman should be all things at once. It should be a drama, a comedy, X-rated, a romantic romp and touching. There are men who believe that sex is a battle of the sexes, a race to the line, who shout out "finished" in triumph after two minutes and 45 seconds of hard and strenuous graft (including foreplay and undressing). These men will never find the perfect woman because they will find someone for whom sex is nothing more than a way to get their partners to buy them a new pair of shoes. Treat sex carefully, my friends. Think of it often as you are wont, but do not discuss it unnecessarily.

What else do women want? According to *The Book of Lists*, Rudolph Valentino, the snake-hipped lover of the silver screen in the Twenties, listed the attributes of his perfect woman thus: "fidelity, the recognition of the supreme importance of love, intelligence, beauty, a sense of humour, sincerity, an appreciation of good food, a serious interest in some art, trade or hobby, an old-fashioned and wholehearted acceptance of monogamy, courage."

Now, I'm not too sure whether this list is in order of importance but, for a man who was supposed to be such a swordsman, the use of "fidelity" and "old-fashioned monogamy" has shattered my image of the bloke. Of course, he could have just been saying it for the chicks, who love that sort of thing, but whatever his reasoning, Valentino has inadvertently, we must presume, come up with the perfect list of things that women want from men – especially the fidelity and monogamy bits. There's nothing in there about having loads of dosh, a fancy car or a Hugo Boss suit, although those were things that a quick poll around with female friends brought up. Others included: brains, humour, affection, a love of Monty Python, unpretentiousness and fun. "It's all about a man who can make a girl's heart soar and keep her happy and in love when the tummy flutters have faded," said one friend. But then another responded with, "Fuck knows," before proceeding to give me a detailed description of fuck knows: "A white knight in shining armour. A man who can cook, clean, iron, head up a business, hold you when you cry and be strong enough to stand up to a head-strong woman." And from a dear but cynical friend: "Someone to take out the garbage and put up shelving." Other attributes included communication, selflessness, good habits, cleanliness, humility, passion, loyalty and honesty.

Quite where they will find a knight who would be willing to sully his armour to cook, clean and take out the rubbish is a mystery. None of them mentioned sex, but you can be sure that it's in there somewhere.

WHAT ATTRACTS US TO DIFFERENT TYPES OF WOMEN?

Er, it's sex, again, actually. Also loads and loads of luck and the odd alcoholic overindulgence. There is no one answer to this question, purely because there is no accounting for taste. The five senses obviously play a part, although you would have to leave taste until at least after you've said hello. Sight, sound, smell and touch are all important and, the first time you meet your perfect woman, beauty is indeed skin deep. Being shallow is no bad thing for the first five minutes. You've never heard your friend say, "My God, look at that ugly girl, I think I will go and talk to her. Perhaps she is Kim Clijsters." You have heard him say: "My God, I'm really hammered and that ugly girl is looking damn fine. I think I shall go accost her. I really hope she isn't Kim Clijsters."

There are so many variants in the early stages of attraction that it would be best if we were to knock out some of the options available out there. I myself have expressed a preference for brunettes over blondes, but then have quite possibly dated more blondes than I have brunettes. An ex-girlfriend who had dark hair dyed it blonde and it felt like I was sleeping with someone new. Luckily I remembered to use her name during sex and saved myself all the fuss that comes with coital clumsiness. Being fussy about what you like is essential at this stage of the search because, before you know it, you could be caught up in a relationship you didn't expect or want, and that's just no good. By all means, have a mental image of the person you are looking for, but do broaden the boundaries. Good chap. I mean, the perfect woman is out there for you, but we all have to make allowances in this modern age. Perfect women come in all shapes, sizes and hair colourings and you should be prepared. As I said before, these could be disguises. The perfect woman for you could be a redhead with a feisty temper and a sharp tongue, she could be missing a leg and be able to drink you under the table, she could even remind you of your mother. It could be in the sultry way she looks at you across the bar (when it's not even happy hour yet), or how she threatens a waiter with physical violence should he mess up her order again, or the simple and obvious fact that she is wearing quite possibly the tightest top in the history of fashion over the perkiest pair of boobs in the history of mammaries.

It could be someone you've known for ages, who you suddenly one day become "aware" of. An ex-girlfriend taught me that word, "aware", when she used it to describe the moment she fell in lust with me, and then to explain to me later how she had become "aware" of someone else and that we were through. I don't much like that word any more, but it's a good one and sums up the moment when you realise that you have found a level of perfection in one person that you hadn't found before. Maybe they should change the word to "beware".

Old friends are a different problem in themselves and will be dealt with in some detail later in this book, but the perfect woman could be involved with one of your friends right now. This could be because familiarity breeds content and that you are settling for the known instead of the unknown. That is an attractive quality, like the special Mickey Mouse blanket you had as a kid or the teddy bear that you just cannot throw out of your bed, not even for the attraction of a satin teddy worn by that nubile young thing you picked up down at the local.

The problem with a lot of searchers is that they set the standards for their perfect women based on what magazines and television tell them they ought to be looking for. As one who has written for magazines about the modern man and bachelorhood and such, a field that is still very much the undiscovered country, I can tell you that much of what you read are sweaty adult masturbation clichés written by lonely old wankers. Not that this is something to be ashamed of, but you want your search for the perfect woman to have some sort of conclusion, don't you? Otherwise you will become no more than a desperate, lonely old wanker, and there are enough of them around.

The readers of *Esquire* magazine voted for what qualities would make up the perfect woman and came to the conclusion that she would have Charlize Theron's legs,

Jessica Simpson's bosom, Jennifer Lopez's bum and the face of Catherine Zeta-Jones. They also said that Britney Spears was the woman they would most pay to see naked (must've been before the pregnancy...). Best breast in the west was Halle Berry, Julia Roberts was the best movie hooker and Ellen Degeneres everyone's favourite lesbian. Angelina Jolie was voted as the sexiest woman alive.

Without, God forbid, being politically correct, these are not good role models for us. Just because you fancy Jolie does not mean that you will find her lookalike out there. Neither will you find another Theron or Simpson. There are, however, plenty of girls with big bums out there who sing badly and get divorced for the fun of it, so a J-Lo doppelgänger is entirely within your reach.

The true seeker of the perfect woman knows that we are attracted to a special something, an aura of dignity spiced up with a streak of sexual and social recklessness inside a comfortable package that is willing to stump up for the next round if you've left your wallet at home again. (A woman who is willing to buy you drinks is always attractive, no matter what.) There will be other factors that will attract you: the peal of her laughter, her curves, the way she puts down your jokes (apparently this means she really, really likes you. If so, then I should be liked a whole lot more than I am) or the way she pushes her hair behind her ears. Attraction: it's a many-splendoured thing. It's also a many-ended thing that requires more investigation.

DIFFERENT TYPES OF WOMEN

Pablo Picasso once famously, or infamously, said that there are only two types of women: "goddesses and doormats". A man who was known to get around, the Spaniard was rumoured to have treated his women rather cruelly, loving them then leaving them when the muse had done her bit for him. He wasn't looking for the perfect woman; he was just looking for someone he could paint without having to shell out for model's fees.

The Kama Sutra names 34 types of women who would be "easy prey" to men, but its descriptions of these women are as convoluted and difficult to understand as its 64 coital positions, 12 non-coital embraces (I can do four of them) and ten different kisses (none of which is the tasty, frozen Italian kind).

Another Greek, Semonides of Amorges, the iambic poet, believed there were ten types of women made by the gods, from animals and the elements. Being a Greek, he believed that only one of them was any good. Indeed, he described them as something of a necessary if beautiful evil, but then he did come from the country that thought dallying with young boys was an accepted part of their education. (A small tip for all travellers: when you go to Athens, do not ask taxi drivers or men in cafés if they are proud they invented sodomy. For some reason they are trying to deny all that botty-action that once went on with gusto and thrusto.)

Semonides wrote that the mind of a woman was made in different ways by the gods. One was from a sow, and this type of woman would leave the house in a mess. Then there was the vixen, a clever, crafty woman not to be trusted because she could hold a conversation; the dog-minded woman was a nosy parker and would argue with her husband all the time; a woman made from the earth didn't know the difference between good and bad and was a bit daft; sea woman was moody; donkey chick was obstinate and not all that fussy; the woman who came from a weasel loved nothing more than sex, but wasn't the best looking and often stole things from her neighbour; those born in the mould of a mare were lazy and only concerned with how good they looked, lashing themselves with perfume and washing twice a day; and the most evil was monkey girl because she was ugly and had no bum, and had a devious mind. The only one he liked was the woman made from the bee, because she had looks, looked after the kids, cleaned the house, was the big cheese down at the Greek book clubs and never gossiped about how crap her man was in the sack.

The Spanish and the Greeks, Mediterranean rednecks it seems, have never been too subtle with their views on women, which has, perversely, meant they have a load more dates than those of us who adhere to the a slightly more polite, more civilised and largely unsuccessful form of finding someone to go out with on a Saturday night. To make oneself attractive to those who like sensitive, new age men, women should be treated with respect and never ever compared to sows, weasels and dogs, unless they have worn your brand new Polo shirt in bed for the second night in a row because it makes them feel closer to you.

There are, however, some women who are doormats because they have become blinded to who they really are, often by men who have tried to shape them into their version of what they want the perfect woman to be. Self-confidence is a stronger turn-on than self-loathing and we valiant men on the search for the perfect woman will not be bribed or swayed by clichéd notions of what she should be. Understood? Marvellous.

Now, what exactly is out there on offer, and is it perfect for us? The following is selection of the type of woman we seek. It is a general road map and by no means all-inclusive, but in each of these types you will find bits and pieces of what does you good.

Slappers, Skanks and Sluts

I had to start with this one because I was shocked and stunned when a female friend of mine used the word "skank" to describe a work colleague who had been promoted ahead of her purely, it seems, because she had the cleavage of an axe-murderer's wife and always undid an extra button or two on her shirt.

When I was a teenager, in the Eighties, the skank was a dance you did when Madness or The Specials were played. When Ska music was at the height of fashion, along with white socks, black shoes, drainpipe black jeans and a T-shirt that had the legend "Free Nelson Mandela (with every packet of Corn Flakes)" emblazoned on the front, we would bend our knees, thrust our alternative little arms forward and bounce like dervishes. Ah, man, we was skanking, I tell ya.

Now, sadly, skanking is a bad, bad thing. It has taken on all the attributes of what a slapper used to be and, before that, a good, old-fashioned slut. Actually, slut is coming back into fashion as the level up from skank. It's a process of graduation: you start off as a slapper, which is both jovial and condescending, then become a skank, which means you are dirty and somewhat promiscuous, while sluts, well, they just bonk for bus change.

In England they have become obsessed with "chavs", the white trash that the tabloids are convinced are binge drinking in city centres, running riot in the housing estates and generally bringing English culture as they know it to a beer-swilling, shaven-headed end. The female version of these "chavs" looks much like Vicky from *Little Britain*: plumpish, pink hooded top, short skirt, Christmas balls for earrings and absolutely no intention to say no when offered sex, particularly if there is a free drink in it for her.

Most of us lost our virginities to girls such as these, and have no right to denigrate them, for they did us a damn big favour. And while the heterosexual female of the species dreams about her first time being with the perfect man in the perfect setting, she is often let down horribly with a fumbled shag in a cramped single bed in a men's residence during Rag week. Virgins very seldom lose their virginity to other virgins, so let us raise up in praise of slappers, skanks and sluts, for they provide the world with no small service. If it wasn't for them, thousands – nay, millions – of young men would be entering the workplace with carpal tunnel syndrome and would spend the formative years of their careers undergoing physiotherapy, costing the economy millions in lost revenue. Next time you chance upon a slapper, thank her for what she does to hold our fragile planet together.

And don't be fooled: there are skanks who can be the perfect woman for you. Promiscuity in a woman is not necessarily a bad thing and, indeed, it would be hypocritical for the majority of men of my acquaintance to claim so. They bring experience and exuberance to the party, and several bedtime (as well as lunchtime and dinnertime) tricks that will amaze and astound your friends should you be a blabbermouth. Slappers tend to become the most monogamous of partners, having had their fill of oats, wild or mild, and will want to settle down (they could use the sleep). And remember, the reputation of a slut is usually blown – ouch! – out of proportion.

How to identify a slapper, skank or slut:

1. Wears one or more of the following: tight jeans, tight T-shirt, tight skirt, tight, partially unbuttoned shirt.
2. Has been blessed with a high metabolism, so has a naturally magnificent body. Jealousy may be one of the reasons she is considered a skank. She may be surgically enhanced if she is over 40.
3. Hair colour is usually blonde, but will be streaked or have that half-and-half, paint-dipped hairstyle that is so popular these days. Will have a decent amount of make-up on to complement her heavy, gold hooped earrings.
4. Is on the pill, but has condoms as back-up because you never know.
5. Drinks alcopops and nails shooters with a delightful screech. Knows a good happy hour when she sees one and has a handful of favourite bars she likes to frequent. Is very rarely there at closing time.
6. Whatever car she drives will have mag wheels, and it will likely have a small dent on the bonnet from when she last got frisky.
7. A smoker (Marlboro Light). She tried to stop by only

smoking after sex but found she was still a 20-a-day girl.

8. Dances to rap songs and sings the lyrics, but sees no irony in mouthing the words "gonna stick it in ma ho".

9. Has a great pick-up line: "Hi. Wanna do a shooter?" The next time you will speak it will be using a deity's name (because you won't be able to remember her's).

10. Works in sales.

Celebrity slappers:
Britney Spears, Victoria Beckham, Jordan, Madonna, Pamela Anderson, Carmen Electra, Monica Lewinsky, most *Big Brother* contestants.

Barbie Dolls

Spotting a Barbie doll is simplicity itself. She is dressed head to toe in branded clothes that match seamlessly, showing off just enough flesh to be flirty, but hiding enough to remain decent. Barbie dolls have the California look, a face that you keep turning around to look at because you know you've seen something similar before, but only in magazines.

I dated such a girl some years ago and the effect she had on others when we went out together was extraordinary and damn fine for my ego. She had the most stunning face, a cute nose, slightly pouty lips, delicate cheek bones and eyes set off by a whisper of mascara. She was, naturally, blonde, with soft, shoulder-length hair that had seen the benefit of years of diligent brushing and had escaped the viciousness of peroxide and the hot African sun. I could almost hear the sharp intake of breath from the men in the room as I put my hand in the small of her back and guided her to our table in the corner. She had a cheeky laugh, was ten years younger than me and had initiated our meeting by letting a colleague know she wouldn't be adverse to me asking her out for a cup of coffee some time. So there we were in a trendy café, me a decade older than her, nervous as hell. Obvious beauty has a tendency to do that to me. I break out in ums and ahs, and say deep things like, "So, what shampoo do you use?" I never got to find out, as we ended a couple of months later.

Going out with my Barbie doll for those 60-odd days was good for my future dealings with other Barbies. I no longer um and ah and ask as to how she keeps her follicles all shiny, strong and full of glorious bounce with nary a frizz in sight. Nope. I have progressed since those heady days and get the drinks in first before blurting out that *Beauty and the Beast* is my favourite fairytale of all time. A hint: do not do this. While a self-deprecating sense of humour turns on some women, the Barbie doll is often quite an ambitious young lass and has big plans for her future. She's heading up the corporate ladder with a turbo-charged smile and often talks about how she is being held back at work by her less talented colleagues. (Now as a sports journalist by trade, I am quite happy with my place on the corporate ladder because the further you climb the less chance you get to drink free beer and watch matches for a living. All the fun is taken out of journalism on the road to the top. It is, therefore, a path less travelled by me, a road I don't want to venture forth on, etc.) And never ask what she sees in you. In fact, never ask this of any woman you are on a date with and whom you cannot believe you have had the most incredible luck to have snagged for an evening. In essence, you are telling the girl that you are not worthy of her and as soon as she gets the hint she will be off before you can tell her that you are a big fan of supermarket anti-dandruff treatments.

On the other hand, some Barbie dolls are quite thick and end up going nowhere in their lives. These are the ones who want to get married quickly and fall into a life of long lunches and tennis dates with other Barbies. Unfortunately, their looks mean that they end up being employed by public relations companies to pretty up launches and such.

The Barbie doll has hidden depths, which will take more than one date to emerge. Despite seeming initially rather prudish, there's a fire a-smoulderin' deep in the heart of that girl and when you give those embers fuel to flame, ready yourself for a rare old time. She will fall in love with you and do things to you in bed (as well as in the lounge, kitchen, office and, for a bit of variety, in the car) to make sure you fall right back in love with her.

How to identify a Barbie doll:

1. Will be dressed in either a matching pant suit or with a shirt emblazoned with the name of the product she is promoting.
2. When you talk, you will find that it is mostly about her: her career, her day at the office, how funny and yet sexy Charlie Sheen is on television. At times like this, you will fully realise that all those rumours about the little Ken doll being gay had some substance. If the real Barbie talked like this she would have neutered the poor sod.
3. Her hair is blonde, almost all of it naturally so. And it's long.
4. Has dated at least one top level sportsman and will tell you that he has been devastated at the news that the two of you are going out. She still has his number on her phone. When you break up, they will get together again.

Believe me on this.

5. Drinks wine sparingly as she really doesn't like to get drunk because she doesn't like to lose control.

6. This is because she is a terrible drunk, and can be either brutally honest when hammered or will throw up in your car, then try to kiss you and ask you if you love her.

7. Drives a sporty hatchback, usually black in colour, or maybe even the pink car her dad bought her when she matriculated with a school-leaving certificate.

8. Was a drum majorette at school and still knows all the twirls and twists.

9. Will be standing near the bar at the latest hotspot in town, or at a table right at the front where everyone can see her.

10. Works in public relations or is about to crack it in the big world of the "media".

Celebrity Barbies:
Cameron Diaz, Reese Witherspoon, Jessica Alba, Jennifer Aniston, Candice Hillebrand, Amor Vittone van der Westhuizen, Patricia Lewis.

Hippie and Kooky Chicks

At university it was cool to be different, except that being different meant you often ended up copying the look and mannerisms of someone else who was different – thus you became exactly the same. At university, Barbie dolls hung out with first-team rugby players and the hippie and kooky chicks hung out with the hippy and kooky guys. Well, some of them did. Others hung around by themselves, glowering at you from Siouxsie and the Banshee-lined eyes, wearing

Doc Martens, drinking beer from the bottle and muttering about the oppression. They, in *Star Wars* terms, were the Dark Side of the hippy chicks; girls who had subverted the power and grace of the universe into a suspicion of all things male and, more importantly for them, pop chart music. They were Darth Vader in make-up and chatting them up was a pointless and painful exercise, even if there may have been untold wonders under that duffle coat and Bauhaus T-shirt.

No, the hippie chick was, and still is, a free spirit of sorts (mainly because there is no such thing as a free spirit, unless, of course, you are a journalist and have access to an open bar. Then your free spirit is a double free spirit with ice). She adheres to no strict definition of what she is and, while hippie and kooky may sound derogatory, they are, in fact, words of some praise. There is a considered aimlessness to the way they dress in that they do not have clothes for set functions; a dress may be worn over a pair of jeans at work, fishnet stockings are combined with a pair of comfortable shoes and a killer leather jacket for a lunch date with friends. But, whatever they wear, the hippie chick always looks comfortable and rarely, despite the odd small joke about how she looks, in her eyes rests a joke that she hopes you get so the two of you can laugh at it together.

The hippie chick likes a drink or two, and is never happier than when she hears the cork being pulled from a bottle of wine, or the hiss of a beer bottle cap being popped. It is something of a mating call for her, that sound, and she may just be of a mind to admit that fact to you when you open the second bottle of wine or knock the head off that fifth beer of the afternoon.

But the main attraction of the hippie chick is in the way

she thinks. She knows how to use technical equipment, for instance, and is usually very good with computers and DVD players. She can throw a ball and quite enjoys going to the gym for the buzz of it all. She has good taste in music and really, really likes sex. She talks about her body and about how "weird my tits look in this dress".

I was triggered by one such beautiful lass in the way she shone her tongue stud at me and ordered me to get to the bar to fetch her another drink or she would lick my lip in public. Oh, the decisions a man has to make, but the bar is a strong motivator, plus we were at a rather posh function. Besides, I got the lick later.

The hippie loves changing things about herself; her hair, her clothes, her car and, sadly, her men. She is a malcontent, never really happy with what she has. More to the point, she does not really know what she wants. This is frustrating, but her whimsical nature is what will draw you to her and, if you fall head over heels for her, it is what will cause her to chase you away. Turn her your way, however, and happiness will surely follow.

How to identify a hippie chick:
1. Will be drinking beer or wine, with occasional forays into whisky, and vodka and bitter lemon.
2. Dress sense can be a little weird at times, but mostly she will wear comfortable clothes: tight strappy tops, cargo pants, utility shoes. As a friend once described it, hippie chicks dress like straight lesbians.
3. Is intelligent with an academic leaning. She will have passed matric and university with distinction, and will still be considering doing a Masters for the fun of it.

4. Her tastes are eclectic, to say the least. She likes most music, from trip hop to classical, trance to the delightful flimsy of the Eighties. Sadly, she can't really dance but she thinks she can.
5. The hippie will not be afraid to tell you what she thinks of you, and she will do it with a smile.
6. Like most women, she does not quite get the whole sport thing, yet she's willing to be active, and will play tennis, squash, cycle or hit the gym hard.
7. Will probably drive a crap second-hand car that she bought from someone in her family who was getting themselves something better. This car will be named, possibly after a beat poet, and will be a mess of empty takeaway packets, study notes and things she meant to return.
8. Hair colour and style change often, sometimes slipping into the aforementioned lesbian look.
9. She is quite a good drunk, although has a tendency to get a little loud and a little flirtatious. Most importantly, she will always buy a round even if she is broke that month.
10. Works in journalism or advertising.

Celebrity hippy chicks:
Winona Ryder, Sandra Bullock, Sheryl Crowe, Karen Zoid.

Career Girls and Career Women

I have never had the, er, good fortune to be matched with a career girl, although I have dated a few Barbie dolls who have come close. I suppose I may have gone out with a handful but, for the life of me, the memory is vague as I write this. Perhaps it will come back to me by the end of the paragraph.

I hope not. There is something rather off-putting about the career girl or career woman for me and, while I can already hear the howls about misogyny and the cackles of the castration brigade, this is not because I fear or am jealous of ambition in women. I find naked ambition, in either sex, a distinctly unattractive thing. Ambition, like its cousin patriotism, is responsible for more broken hearts and bodies than they know or care about, yet there are some people who find power attractive, just as there are some people who think putting their appendages inside small, hairy mammals is a turn-on.

I don't hold anything against career women (and after writing this will probably never ever hold anything near one of them) because, as the saying goes, some of my best friends are career girls. Some of them have fallen up the corporate ladder by mistake rather than design, and have found themselves well-suited to the pressures, demands and, most particularly, the rewards that come with being in a corporation that pays the going rate and above. Others have walked all over people to get up the ladder, leaving a trail of bruised careers in their wake and creating plenty of enemies along the way.

Of course, some girls are just wannabe career women, just as there are (we hope) wannabe sluts, slappers and skanks. They will dress the part, usually head to toe in black, a serious colour for a serious person, and will talk up the part, but are nothing more than pimped-up secretaries (which is, to be cruel, nothing more than another section of the skank brigade). If you get your jollies from dating powerful women, then beware, you may be getting yourself into far less than you hoped for with these girls. If you wake up and she's doing an inventory of your room and wants to spend the day looking at the yacht you bragged about last night, then ask her for her business card. If she gives it to you freely, she's a fraud. The truly powerful bints have no need of business cards; they wear their power like a mink stole.

Sleeping with career girls on the way up can actually come back to haunt you, unless, of course, you marry her then reap the benefits of her wealth. A good friend of mine is married to such a woman and, while he still has his job, he is more than happy being a house husband. He looks after their two kids while she travels the country doing, er, business things.

So, here's the thing about career girls from my sad perspective: a lot of them are dead boring, have little time for love in their lives and are far too structured to enjoy themselves or the ones they are with. If you are dead boring, have no time and live a structured life, perhaps this is the very woman for you. If you are a gold-digger, the same applies. Good luck to you. I've just remembered that I did indeed date a few career girls and women and, believe me, you're a braver man than me.

How to identify a career girl/woman:
1. What stage of her career she is at will define what she drinks. If she is starting out, then it will be white wine; if she is with her male colleagues, it will be a single malt on the rocks, just to show she can hang with the blokes; if she has made it to the top, she will drink whatever the hell she wants.
2. Her clothes will be a statement because they have to be; usually black pants and jacket, she will show a bit of

cleavage for the lads because every little bit helps and because she can.

3. Has an MBA and is not afraid to use it at the bar.

4. Carries a Blackberry, a PDA and one of those cellphones that opens up to reveal a laptop and a wet bar. At least one of those appliances will be in her hands at all times and she will look at them constantly, just in case.

5. Strangely enough, she may be alone at the bar, primarily because she is waiting for someone to meet her, possibly a business client. She is confident enough to arrive at the bar first to gain the upper hand on her client.

6. Drinks soda water at lunch and asks for mineral water by brand.

7. Young career girls try to show off by telling you how much they mean to the business and they will tell you how unappreciated they are by their bosses. If you are callous, hold their hands and tell them you appreciate them. You'll have them in bed in no time.

8. Changes her car annually, and will have a BMW: perhaps a Z4 for the city, or an X3 for going up to the trout farm on weekends.

9. The career woman does not usually get drunk, although the career girl often does. The woman will be more expressive in the sack and will have the toys to prove it. Keep spare batteries in your car just in case.

10. Works in, um, business doing, er, business stuff.

Celebrity career girls/women:
Martha Stewart, Delia Smith, Cherie Blair.

Other Types of Perfect Women

I fear that the end of this first chapter has come upon me in a heated rush and I have little space for the myriad women out there. Fear not. In my research I have come across many different types and they will appear in this handy guide in one or more of the following chapters. What I have found is that the types tend to overlap slightly, although the stereotypes do mostly remain true.

There is the athletic girl, a female from whom you may have to hide in a fitness protection programme after she gets hold of your love handles and attempts to rip them off. The marrying woman is on the lookout for a husband and has been planning her marriage since she was five years old (a friend tells me that most women are like this, but he is a chauvinist). Then there is the foreign woman, the sister of a friend, the ex-girlfriend, the set-up, the... oh, the list goes on and on. Believe this, my friends, there is a perfect woman out there for you. She just doesn't know it yet.

2

BARS. ARE THEY ALL THEY'RE CRACKED UP TO BE?

I **love bars.** Absolutely love them. When I travel abroad, the first thing I do in a new country is check in and ask the doorman at the hotel to point me in the direction of the nearest local so I can get a feel of the country I have landed in. It's a simple and revealing process: you sit down, order a beer and pay for it. In fact, I can say "Large beer, please" in every single language in the world. All I do is point at the nearest beer tap, make a gesture that says big and pay over my recently converted money. While some economists use the "Big Mac" index as an indication of the expensiveness or cheapness of a nation's standard of living, I use the "Big Beer" index. It's a great research methodology. You get to sit down while you do it, create a little bit of a beer buzz into the bargain and, if you are a clever and wily sports journalist, you can push it through with your other expenses as a "colour" article on how, well, colourful the locals are.

I love bars almost as much as I fear dating and yet the two are far too intertwined for their own good. Dating and drinking go well together because of the rather obvious ability of booze to smooth rough edges and break down social, emotional and physical barriers. Dating and drinking, as with drinking and driving, or even dating and driving (which is called prostitution in some countries, although it really should be called dating and parking) is not a very safe thing to do and, while not always encouraged, sometimes you just can't avoid it. My search for the perfect woman has been partially fuelled by the odd drink or two dozen and while this has sometimes been spectacularly successful, it has also been known to cause its fair share of problems. A woman I had a desperate crush on once took a friend aside in a bar where we were all partying rather heavily after a rugby test, and asked about me and where my life was going. My friend, on his seventh double Jameson's and ice, was nonplussed by the question and asked why, to which she declared, "Because I really like him, but he just drinks far too much."

Unfortunately, for the both of us, she was the sort of girl who couldn't handle her booze all that well and did not like to relinquish any control over herself. She once called me up to tell me she was at a bar with her cousin and would love to see me. She sounded a bit slurry on the phone, but I took this to be because of the reggae music that was pumping in the background and, later that night, after I had done my sports editor's duty and put *The Sunday Independent* to bed, I rushed across town to hook up with her. As I parked the car and was walking to the bar, a strange number appeared on my cell phone. It was her, calling from her cousin's phone, because she had dropped hers in the toilet, where she had gone to throw up the several shooters her kind cousin had forced upon her. "I don't want you to see me like this," she wailed. As I had absolutely no wish to see her like that, never mind kiss a girl who had just regurgitated her food and was drunk enough to flush her phone, I did the honourable thing by turning around, hopping in my car and heading down to my local to meet up with mates for a good couple of drinks before closing time.

The girl called me the next day to apologise profusely and got a little annoyed when I started laughing at her, telling her that it was fine and that it had happened to everyone of us at some time or another.

"But," she trembled, "I don't want you to think of me as a silly young girl." Which reminded me that she had taken her sweet time about telling me how old she was, chiefly because she was ten years younger than me. It was a massive thing for her, as she hadn't ever gone out with a man that much older than her. I told her, gently and with my fingers crossed, that there was no way that I could ever think of her as a silly young girl, knowing that thinking of her as a young and very beautiful girl was the very thing that had attracted me to her in the first place. She never drank much when we were together after that, strangely enough. No matter; I made up for the two of us, which, as I have already mentioned, she saw as rather a major flaw in my make-up. I did manage to put her in a catch-22 situation once, though. I got memorably drunk with a prominent retired sporting personality at a function she was organising and convinced him that she was the best function organiser I have ever dated. He did not need to know that she was the only function organiser I had ever gone out with, but she still got some more work because of it. Drinking works in mysterious ways, doesn't it?

Bars are good places for the incurably shy to find a woman who may not be the perfect woman but will be a start, or even a pleasant distraction, on the journey to finding the Holy Maid. I myself have been pounced upon by women in bars, not because of my outstanding good looks, generosity with my wallet or even because of the fact that I am under 40 (where have I heard that before?), but because the women in question thought I had "game" and responded to it in the manner they thought most appropriate. "Game" was a word I heard for the first time a few years ago. It was used in the same breath as "skank" and "slapper", incorrectly so, I was to learn, for having "game" is, apparently, having the ability to successfully chat up a young lady or put "moves" on her in such a way that she finds you attractive enough to want to go on a date with you.

I have heard men talk about losing their "game" in the same way that sportsmen speak of searching for form on the field. Chatting up women is like being in the "zone" for them, and should they lose the thread of their "game" they will keep barging away at the defence until they find it again. It is, apparently, a confidence thing and the search for the perfect woman is all about confidence.

DIFFERENT TYPES OF "GAME"

The Bad Boy Game

I have several friends who are from a town on the far East
Rand, where, it seems, they have a university in teaching
young men how to chat up ladies, take them home for a jolly
good seeing to and never speak to them again. Now some of
you may think that this says less about their skills and more
about the type of female who lives on the East Rand, but
you would be wrong. My friends have been highly successful
outside of what one might call their rightful social strata,
and have chalked up many successes.

When we were younger there were a group of four of
us who would go out together. Nowadays, young people,
bizarrely infatuated with American rap culture, might call
us a "crew" (they might also say we were going back to our
"crib", then call each other "beeeyatch" and "dog", while
showing off their underpants and walking as though they
were wearing concrete boots), but we decided to name
ourselves the F.O.L.D. This was short for Francois Oldham
Land Development, a company we made up to impress
women into thinking we were rich, young men going places.

It was also a joke we had had at university that anyone who
was not allowed to come out and drink with us, for whatever
reason, was said to have been lost to the "Fold". Once out,
he could come back and we would accept him back into the
bosom of the Fold.

After university we worked the F.O.L.D. hard when the far
East Rand boys had worked a few girls into our crowd. One
of us would be the managing director, another the financial
manager and the other the project manager. I, because of my

journalism background, was always designated as being in charge of marketing and public relations. I wasn't entirely happy with that as I wanted to be the MD some nights, but we all choose our paths and have to live with them.

Needless to say, the other three had a higher success rate than I, possibly because I just couldn't keep up the F.O.L.D. persona and would start laughing halfway through after a few beers and let the cat out of the bag. I am not a great liar (though I can tell a mean fib, usually to editors on deadline).

When the F.O.L.D. story got old and we all tired of it, the bad boy "game" was found to work best and was put to good use. Being from the East Rand and driving a 16-valve Golf GTi was as clichéd as you are likely to get, but it had a James Dean charm to it and a lot of women, sadly and strangely enough, are still and forever will be attracted to the bad boy. In a nightclub after a rugby test, one of our group, now since passed away, who had the East Rand accent and the 16-valve charm (this was the same guy of whom a rather snotty and chubby rich girl once asked, "Where did you get that accent?" "Brakpan," he replied. "Where did you get that fat butt?"), hooked up with a girl who thought he was an international rugby player. He had shaved his hair that morning, using the number one blade. To this day there is a girl in the northern suburbs who thinks she slept with James Small, and yet my friend was far taller and looked nothing like the Springbok wing. What she doesn't know won't hurt her, unless, of course, she buys this book and her friends remember her bragging about being on a wing and a player.

Watching some of my friends make off with women through the "bad boy" game has bothered me for some time. I did some research into it and found that there was a website by a gentleman called Joseph Edwards on how to attract women. The advert read: "You befriend a woman in the hopes of turning it into a relationship, but then you get stuck in the dreaded 'Friends Zone'. You see one jerk after another walk off with the women you want, while you're stuck being the 'nice guy'." I almost sent off for his book, *The Art of Approaching*, but, like the Charles Atlas course to change my body from that of a 90-pound weakling into one that only superheroes possess, with sand-kicking skills thrown in, I was sceptical and had reservations about sending $80 into cyberspace.

But part of me wanted to be a bad boy. In the throes of trying to convince an ex-girlfriend, who had dumped me for a man politely described by his two ex-wives, ex-fiancée and other friends as a "piece of self-absorbed shit", that we could make it work, I asked her whether she would have stayed if I'd treated her badly. She paused for a second or two before spouting forth a series of denials then professing that she had loved me because I was such an "understanding" and "sensitive" guy. Understanding? Sensitive? Me? "Yes," she said quietly, "you're a nice guy."

The Nice Guy Game

I was accused of having this by the boss of a girl I was dating. She, ostensibly a friend, was not happy that I was seeing her employee because she thought it was a conflict of interest (the girl was in public relations and went well beyond the call of duty to be nice to this particular journalist) and eventually poisoned her against me with a sly campaign of slander and half truth. The boss told me she had been watching us journalists in a bar during a tournament we were covering and had seen a pattern emerging. One of our colleagues was a flatterer, the other a bad boy and me, well, I played the nice guy.

I explained to the unbeliever that this was because I was, indeed, a nice guy who only wanted to do nice things to her employee. I left out the bit about the two of us having already done nice things to each other, as I didn't need any more aggravation, and let her explain how the nice guy act worked. Apparently I don't use lines, I am not overly touchy, am attentive, listen well, laugh at jokes and flirt gently. If truth be told – and this is a book in which I have been asked to tell the truth so I will endeavour to do so – I talk to women thus not because it is a process that I have worked out as being successful, but because I am innately shy, which, apparently, is just another part of my act. The "nice guy" waits for the girl to make the first move, usually out of frustration or possibly because she is the mothering type and thinks the little lost boy needs a bit of a kick-start.

I have had limited success with this act.

After doing the nice guy act for the best part of a month, I was jumped by a colleague outside a bar in which the two of us had been drinking since lunchtime (journalism is very forgiving of the long lunch, an art that is being lost to the world. Fear not, some of us still keep the tradition going.), which kick-started a relationship that lasted two months and made the office decidedly uncomfortable when it came to an end. We also kissed in front of the parking attendant and a bemused beggar. It all seemed a little surreal and perhaps then I should have twigged that trouble lay ahead, but I was drunk and liquor does strange, if delightful, things to a man.

The night before my birthday a few years ago I was in

my local with my mates when a young, pretty girl sat down next to me and told me, without any shame, that she was celebrating getting out of rehab for a little problem she had with the devil's dandruff. As only a nice guy can, I bought her a drink to celebrate and then wondered how in the name of Christ I was going to escape her. After an experience in a bar the week before when an older, drunk woman and her equally slaughtered buddy had approached a friend and me, I was exceptionally wary of ignoring her. I had done this to drunk number one as she tried to get me to buy her a drink and then take me home or to the back of her car, whichever came first. When that didn't work, I had asked her to leave me alone – and received a rather impressive bitchslap for my trouble. The manager walked across to us with a smirk on his face and, with his hands on the women's shoulders, removed them from the bar, telling them that, as it was the third time that week that the pair of them had hit a man, they were now permanently barred. The rest of the bar giggled at me as I turned back to the counter and my friend wasted no time in telling all of my other friends that I had been "fucked up by a drunk chick in a bar".

But back to Miss Rehab… Her friend sat down next to my inebriated buddy and tried to fix her eye on him. Unfortunately her eyes were so badly squint that one looked at right angles to the other: she looked like a pissed chameleon, a defect my not-so subtle friend picked up immediately and asked: "Jesus, how hammered are you, luvvie?"

Undeterred, she sat on as Miss Rehab left for a toilet break to possibly powder her nose in that special way that girls out of rehab have a need to do, fixed me with one of her eyes and warned me that her friend was unstable and prone to having wanton sex with totally strange men. I took her words under advisement and was suitably wary and interested when Miss Rehab sat back down beside me and generously bought herself a drink from my pile of change that had gathered on the bar in front of me. As the clock hit midnight and my birthday came around, the barman rushed over a birthday shooter and congratulated me on having lived so well for so long. As Spike Milligan would say, I laughingly felled him with a right cross. Miss Rehab put her hand on my thigh, whispered happy birthday in my ear and proceeded to shove her tongue down my throat. Being the nice guy I am, I reciprocated, allowing my tongue to be swirled around our mouths in a quite expert and not at all unpleasant manner, smiled, kissed her again, thanked her and excused myself to go to the toilet. Not even the potential offer of wanton sex can hold back the tide that comes with the drinking of many beers.

As I tend to do in toilets in bars after a certain time of the evening, I stood and looked at myself in the mirror, wondering just how thick my beer goggles were and how rosy her wine spectacles were, checked my hair was as silly looking as ever and prepared to put on a swanky swagger (which is about three beers away from being a wanky stagger) as I walked back to my space at the bar counter next to her. When I came back she was gone. Perhaps I was too nice, although my friends castigated me for being uncool. Sucking face while sitting at the bar counter is almost as cool as vomiting on your shoes or refusing to buy a round and, now that I had done the worst of this trifecta, I got whatfor.

When we moved the party to the bar next door, she was

seated at the bar next to a bemused-looking and titillated man. We found ourselves in adjacent urinals later in the evening and he was giggling to himself about the bird he had just met. She had told him that she had arrived back in the country after several years abroad, where she had hung around with a rock band we had vaguely heard of. It sounded like a damn fine story to me, just the sort of girl I would want to have wanton sex with. Damn, I thought, when I got home later that night, alone and wondering if I would ever get to have some of that new-fangled Chinese won ton sex I had heard about. I had just been played. The girl had game, man, she had spun us a classic "bad girl" yarn.

The Tortured Soul Game

Oh, hang on, I think I lied earlier. I have indeed tried to put on "game", because I am sure I have definitely tried this technique on women. In my defence it's usually done when I'm three sheets to the wind and of a wont to be deep. Except that I am most palpably not deep at those moments; I am shallow and pathetic and should be sent home taking my ill-of-the-world carrying shoulders with me.

Pretending to be the misunderstood artist is not difficult. Be quiet, be moody, nurse your stout or whisky (lager and wine are not really tortured drinks). Malt was burnt to make stout, a metaphor for the burnt state you find yourself in, and whisky, well that's strong, which you are trying to be despite the aforementioned burnt state you find yourself in. Now, this state can be either because you are a tortured artist-type person, or because you have just been dumped, the latter being the second-most used and by far the most acceptable reason for drinking since the invention of brewing and distilling.

The artist game is harder than it looks to pull off. You can wear the distressed black jeans and frumpy shirt and you can be reading Jack Kerouac, but if you don't have a decent distressed look on your dial, then, mate, you are going into play only half-dressed. The artist has to be distressed to kill and, because this is a phase that most males grow out of after our first or second years of university, it is a game that seems to have been stuck in a time warp, as it doesn't have that high a success rate. Most tortured artists chuck it all in for the bad boy game, but for others, for the Jedi masters of this art, there is – with apologies to Yoda, the only wise man who ever had a hand up his bum – no try, there is only do or do not.

Beginner artists fail because they aren't actually artists at all. Or they're just not clever. They so badly want to be intellectuals that they take upon themselves an air they actually don't understand. At university, during a journalism tutorial, we were asked about the influence of western culture on South African youth culture. One of those, a member of that group cruelly called bungees (because they tried so hard to be different and alternative that they all ended up being the same, establishing cliques almost as stifling as those of the rugger buggers they so despised), said he felt that he didn't think so because South Africans were forging their own culture. I looked him up and down, from his John Lennon glasses to his Mod-influenced army jacket, his tapered jeans and army surplus shirt and laughed. The room, 70 per cent bungee and female, stared me down, as I had challenged their leader. "Dude," I turned to the hip tutor, "look how he's dressed. He so badly wants to be John Lennon or Paul Weller it's not funny." The bungee groupies gasped, although two of them looked as though they had just woken up from a deep sleep. As the intellectually-bereft often do, the Lennon wannabe shouted me down with pseudo-Marxist nonsense and a few quotes I found out later were from Hunter S Thompson. I wish I had had the wherewithal to tell him that the good doctor of gonzo journalism was one of the greatest comic writers of all time. Mind you, some girls say they are looking for a man to make them laugh. What I did say was: "Everyone has an act, china, and yours is a poor copy of the original." Later that night, down at the sadly defunct Cathcart Arms in Grahamstown, the slighted pseudo-intellectual glowered at me over his pint of Raven's Stout. He was surrounded, I noticed, by fewer of his groupies than the night before.

The most successful of the tortured souls are those who have had a bus crash of a break-up and can use it to make a woman feel sorry for him – sufficiently so to get her into bed with him, or at least on to a second date. In his exceptionally funny autobiography, *CAD: Confessions of a Toxic Bachelor*, former *New York Times* and *Newsweek* entertainment writer Rick Marin explains that he used the break-up of his brief and desperate marriage as a line during dates. The first words of his book are:

> *"Yeah, I don't really like to talk about it."*
> *I peeled off my glasses and peered myopically in the general direction of the woman I was trying to impress.*
> *"Talk about what?" asked Chloe, my elusive and enigmatic date, taking a swig of cognac.*
> *I gazed deeply into what might have been her left ear and pulled out the only juicy detail on my emotional resumé.*

"My marriage."
"Oh," she said, eyes widening.

Four pages later, a bottle of Tio Pepe and a few hours after
he brought up his marriage for the first time, Chloe (name
changed to protect the gullible. In fact, Marin has changed all
the names and identifying details of the women in his book.
Perhaps I should have done the same.) feels emotionally
close enough to Marin to sleep with him and then ask if they
can spend the day together. He, after noting that she has
nipple hair and in deference to her request for "honesty", tells
her he is busy (it was a Sunday, as I remember) and shows
her the door.

He tries this technique more than once in the book, with
more hits than misses, and even has the balls to attempt it
on the woman he thinks is the one, the perfect woman for
whom we all seek and the reason for the writing of this book.
She puts on his glasses, then takes them off and gets some
intense eye contact going. "I was married once, you know,"
she tells him. "You *were*?" replies Marin. His perfect woman
takes in his shocked expression: "No, I'm doing *you*." As the
wise man would say, you're nicked, my son.

The tortured soul game is a high-risk one because at some
stage you are going to have to stop being the victim. If you
have nowhere to go after that, nothing more than a line or
a quote from a book you haven't yet finished, then you are
in trouble. And woe betide you if you meet a woman who
knows that the true tortured artist/soul sucks up his pain
and keeps quiet.

The 'I Think I Might Be Gay' Game

Again, this is a dangerous ploy to play because it puts you on a sexual knife edge, which could swing either way, so to speak. Act too gay and you could find yourself with a "fag hag" on your hands who thinks it's cool to have gay friends because she feels safe that they won't try to hit on her. Don't act gay enough and you won't be in the slightest bit interesting to them at all, just a soft bloke.

The emergence of the metrosexual has seen this act grow in popularity, although many metrosexuals are still in the bathroom closest and refuse to talk to other men about what moisturisers they use and on what parts of their bodies. Indeed, if anyone in some of the mobs I hang out with were to speak of the glories of aloe as opposed to the cooling powers of menthol, he would find himself speaking in an uncomfortable silence. Some of the kinder closet moisturisers might later put a comradely arm around his shoulder and tell him that things would be all right – but to keep it zipped, okay.

In Barcelona, the gay clubs are full of straight people because they are the best clubs and tend to stay open until 10am the next day. Their motto is: "We don't mind straight people, as long as they act gay in public." Gay is the new straight, people.

On pickupguide.com (the Maniac High's Pick Up Girls Guide and Seduction Website. It is presented in conjunction with Fast Seduction 101. Maniac High is a guy who lives in Tokyo and "likes to pick up chicks".), I stumbled across a post from a fellow who said that he had found considerable success with acting gay because of an article he had read in *Playboy* (see, there are people who read that magazine for the articles). Apparently the writer of the article spent much of his time acting gay and "nailed some of the most elite models and actresses in NYC". The "gay guy" took his act to extreme measures and immersed himself in the gay community just so he could add to his list of scores with women. The poster of the comment sounded rather homophobic and was quite proud of the way in which the author had fooled gays because he "banged chicks left and right. Woman who hung with this crowd (gay fashion designers, hairstylists, etc) never suspected he wasn't gay and would hang around him because they felt he was safe. Also he was into hairstyling, art, fashion, make-up, etc. He could talk for hours with woman about clothes, make-up, etc. He did over 2 000 lays living this lifestyle."

The poster goes into detail about how he has a friend (don't we all) who is the greatest pick-up artist he knows in his area. In his area? That begs the question as to whether some men see picking up women as a competition. As they obviously have websites and talk about it, do they have clubs in which they compete to be the club champion? Does the club champion then go to a regional fuck-off to see how many shags they can get in a week? Would it be done on quantity alone, or would they have a set of judges marking them out of ten on technique, time and quality of women pulled? Does sleeping over win you points or is it considered a waste of valuable pulling time? Hey, if figure skating and synchronised swimming are considered legitimate sports, then surely "picking up" can be added to the list?

Anyway, I've got sidetracked again... Oh yes, the best pick-up artist in the area. Well, apparently, he's extremely successful with the ladies but, our new friend worries, he has the most effeminate voice. "I can't believe it. He talks like a girl. He don't look like one. In fact he's very macho looking but still. He's like talking to a chick and he sounds like a girl. Even when talks to me he sounds like a girl. I almost thought he was gay. He'd talk about his relationships, girlfriends, clothes, etc… just like a chick. It made me sick because on the outside he looks manly enough but his tonality is so different from his looks." (Sic, by the way.)

I've never met this lad, but I think I know the type. Think David Beckham and that really soft voice of his. Mind you, Mike Tyson also has a soft voice, but he doesn't talk about relationships and clothes, unless he's trying to convince a jury that the sex was consensual and that he didn't rip anyone's clothes off nor did he mean to hit them as hard as he could. But Becks, well there's a man who knows how to dress, moisturises himself silly, knows, allegedly, how to SMS bisexual girls into a frenzy and could have his pick of women.

Acting gay is bringing your feminine side to the fore in a big way. You have to have the ability to speak to a woman like another woman would. In the same way that lesbians who have experienced straight sex say the best sex they have ever had was with other women because they know what makes them tick, so do women know how to chat each other up without it ever seeming cheesy. Very few men can master this art unless they are either very lucky or have spent a large part of their childhood surrounded by sisters. Women know the nuances, when another woman is on the prowl, how to bring up sex, how to chat about clothes, make-up, relationships, that kind of thing. The last word on this from our slightly homophobic pick-up artist:

"I frequently act gay and effeminate; talk about clothes, make-up, boys and be one of the girls. I practise these skills and women keep coming back for more. I have not experienced this much popularity with woman before. In the past I was like a shark swimming around and devouring some unsuspecting duck. Now I am trying to relate to woman on a whole different level. I'm making this type of behavior around woman more natural. It is powerful, it works and I what I love most is I'm not doing the old games that I used to use on woman that left them feeling dirty, degraded and used." [Once again, sic.]

Hmmm, a changed man. Perhaps there is hope for us all if we act a little gayer.

BAR ETIQUETTE

"Candy is dandy, but liquor's quicker." – Dorothy Parker

As someone who does not have all that much truck with norms and traditions, I've never been one for too much etiquette, though I do believe there are some elements of politeness and manners that should be adhered to, not just when on a date or when hoping to meet that special someone.

I am not a great dater, as I may have mentioned before. I get horrifically nervous, which is why I like meeting women in bars or anywhere else that will let me stand up and drink beer. Should I ever find a place that lets me lie down and drink beer, then I will move there, but until that magic day comes, anywhere close to 90 degrees and vertical is as good as any angle to have a drink at. Being on your back in a bar, however, is not going to have the women running to you, unless, of course, you are there because you've just taken a fearful thumping from two gorillas because you were defending the lady's honour. Then she will, hopefully, buy you a drink after helping you to your feet and telling you how brave she thinks you are.

When I trawl through my list of married or divorced friends, or those with common-law wives (an unfortunate term and, herewith, a lesson: do not, as I did, ask your friend's common-law wife just how common she was. I found out.), I find that most of them met their partners in bars and after a few drinks. It must be said, however, that the vast majority of my friends do like a drink a little more than your average Joe and that the odds of them meeting women in bars are considerably lower than for others. Actually, they were probably even money to meet their spouses in bars. One even met his spouse in a bar a couple of months after he had married her. It was just a pity for her and a rather expensive error by him that he was with his girlfriend at the time.

Perfect women are thick on the ground in bars, but to view the bar as a hunting ground is to do the institution a great disservice. It could also possibly sully and tarnish the feel of a bar if you play out one or more of the previously-mentioned games in them. There are rules in bars, strict rules, after all: these places sell a legal drug, a lowerer of inhibitions so potent that many of you reading this will have lost your virginities to it and are still trying to expunge the memories of that fateful, fumbling night from your memories. Some of you may even have no memories of that night at all. Myself,

I remember it well. I never told the young lady involved that it was my first time, although I'm sure she suspected it and, even if she didn't, the two of us had had our fill of enough schnapps, beer and the remnants of some exotic German digestif from her father's liquor cabinet for her not to care a monkey's. Back then, as a good Irish Catholic, I knew little of the etiquette of these things and scarpered shortly after the deed was done in case God was watching and would make me blind, strike me down and make my palms and other bits hairy.

Since then I have learnt to be a gentleman, not always perfect, but a gentleman, nevertheless. It's the harder, rockier path on the search for the perfect woman, but there are basic laws of style and decency that should not be broken, yet are trespassed upon by those who take the easier path and hit upon women indiscriminately and with no class. A quick lesson in how to conduct the search and yet appear as though you are not doing so is in order.

THE CHAT-UP LINE

"Sex is better than talk. Talk is what you suffer so you can get to sex." – Woody Allen

I, myself, have never used a line. Why? Because I would be far too embarrassed to do so and, because I am such a shy, retiring and rather insecure chap, I just know I would get laughed at. Would I have used a line if I were brave enough? Um, possibly, but it would have been along the lines of something by Oscar Wilde or the good doctor, Hunter S.

Something witty, clever and devastating. Oh, hang on, I've just remembered: I have actually used a line – and it didn't work either.

In an upmarket club one night, out with a group of friends who had convinced me that this would be a good place for me to extend myself and meet women "out of my league", I proceeded to get a little out of my head. They had, for whatever reason, the Fashion Channel on the dozen or so televisions around the bar and I, after having focused on the most delicate beauty nearest me, ripped out one of Mr Wilde's finest: "You know, fashion is a form of ugliness so intolerable that we have to alter it every six months."

"Yes," she smiled and fingered my collar, getting me all hot and bothered under it, "but, then why are your clothes and your hair still six months in arrears."

I was ready for this. "But I'm six months in advance. This was cool and happening 12 years ago. What goes around comes around in the fashion world, you know. Yellow replica Liverpool Football Club shirts with Redknapp on the back will be the hot, retro item in a month or so."

She leaned close, her mouth near my ear. "Yes, but right now it's ugly and you are intolerable," she whispered before walking away, leaving me blushing and taking an unusual interest in the television screen. Fuck Oscar Wilde. You should never trust an Irishman who played the "I think I'm straight" game with such gay abandon. But, still, he did give me a great comeback in situations such as these.

"Yeah, sweetheart, but most women are so artificial that they have no sense of art. Most men are so natural that they have no sense of beauty. So there!" I belted at her disappearing back, and followed up with: "We are all of us living in the gutter, but some of us are looking at the stars."

She stopped and turned. I had her. "Shut the fuck up, will you?"

So that you do not suffer this embarrassment in the future, herewith, courtesy of insult.net, are a selection of lame lines and their put-downs:

Are you happy?
I was.

Bond. James Bond.
Off. Piss off.

Ever wanted to deflower a virgin?
Nope.

Go on, don't be shy: ask me out.
OK, get out.

Got a light?
Yes thanks.

Hello.
Goodbye.

Mind if I take your picture?
Where to?

Please take a seat.
Where to?

Queuing is so boring, don't you find?
It is now.

Um, hello.
Oscar Wilde, I presume?

What sign were you born under?
No entry.

Why not be original and say yes?
No.

"Yes" is my favourite word. What's yours?
No.

You look like a model.
No, I'm real.

Your face or mine?
His.

You're cute.
My cute what?

You're irresistible.
You're resistible.

You've got great boobs.
So have you.

And a few more terrible lines, the difference being that I've actually heard these used in bars:

Do you have a map? I just keep on getting lost in your eyes. I'd marry your dog just to get in the family.

Would you touch me so I can tell my friends that I've been touched by an angel?

Hello. Cupid called. He says to tell you that he needs my heart back.

Excuse me, do you have your phone number? I seem to have lost mine.

That's a nice outfit. It would look great crumpled up on my floor.

If you were a pair of pants I'd wear you out!

You must be a thief, because you stole my heart from across the room.

Your lips look so lonely. Would they like to meet mine?

If I could rearrange the alphabet, I'd put U and I together. (According to South African cricketer Jacques Kallis, this is his best mate, South African wicketkeeper Mark Boucher's favourite line, although I think he may have been telling a little fib.)

Hey. Want to go halvies on a baby?"

The Japanese, as always, have done extensive psychological and sociological research to find the ultimate chat-up line. Near the end of 2004, the *Times of London* reported that the only country to be attacked with nuclear bombs had come up with what they thought would be a weapon of mass destruction in the war of the bars. They used calculations, based on "word triggers" and the skewed Japanese interpretation of western culture.

The sentence is: "rainen no kono hi mo issho ni waratteiyoh", which means, in a direct translation: "This time next year, let's be laughing together." Bugger me, if it doesn't sound clever, but it can never work in the West. It sounds too contrived, too practised for anyone to be able to pull it off. The Japanese, though, like Baldrick in Blackadder, believe it to be a line more cunning than a fox who was the professor of cunning at Cunning University. The line, ostensibly to be used by men more than women (Japan, it seems, is not that liberated yet), intrigues me. There are three word triggers, apparently, which are like the subconscious advertising that was banned in movie theatres in the United States all those years ago. (Remember, the ads that made you want to buy hot dogs and soft drinks during the intervals? No? See, it worked. Fetch me a Coke, boy.)

Here's the explanation:

Saying "this time next year" implies that the lad is not just there for a shag, but is interested in a long-term love contract. "Together" is another trigger, apparently saying that their love will still be abloom the following year. "Laughing" gives the line "softness" and implies that Mr Sakamoto is full of fun and even a little cheeky. And because there is this sense of cleverness and cheek, even the shyest of lads will be able to walk away with some honour should his geisha give him short shrift.

It seems the Japanese need every encouragement they can to get their young men and women into bed. "The discovery comes in the nick of time for Japan, whose fertility rate continues to lurch downwards to record lows," reported the *Times*. "Observers have spotted numerous signs that Japanese romantic life is taking a beating from long working hours and the nervousness of men around increasingly successful women. Incidents of women buying pets has quadrupled over the past year and occupancy rates at the country's 18 000 "love hotels" have plummeted. The chat-up line is for any context, but it favours particular situations. It works extremely well, for example, if used to chat up someone you have seen a few times in the office but never spoken to. It is good for the coffee shops, but less effective in noisy bars. Its perfect application would be in Japan's many "pulling places" – spots in each town where, by tacit public agreement, any woman who pauses for more than a few seconds is fair game.

The lucky sods. Imagine being able to wait around the town square to size up the talent on display. It would be like internet dating, but without the ADSL costs or the potential of being lied to online. *Times* reader Laura Gibson wasn't convinced it would work, though: "The Japanese population will die out if all the men resort to this line. It sounds like a line designed by men who have no sense of humour and who think that all women are stupid and desperate."

I find it pleasing that the Japanese believe the line will not work in bars. There are only some lines that work in bars in the search, good readers. And these are:

"Can I buy you a drink?"

"Hi, my name is Kevin." (Or another name, even your real one.)

"You're obviously not a Manchester United fan, are you?" (To woman wearing Manchester United shirt.)

As a rule, however, lines do not work. Some perfect women, however, are not perfect and will fall for the most inane things. Such are the motives and mysteries of the female of the species.

WHAT TO DRINK

"I hate to advocate drugs, alcohol, violence, or insanity to anyone, but they've always worked for me."
– Hunter S Thompson

It took me all of two weeks after I started drinking before I found I liked the taste of beer. It will take me until two seconds before I die to lose my taste for beer. Beware, though: what you drink will define you, and you want that definition to be a good one. An ex-girlfriend used to kiss me good night after we had been out for drinks (and I had convinced her that it would be a good idea for us to end the evening with a bang) and would say, "Beer breath." That was my cue to rush to the bathroom, brush my teeth and counter with "Cigarette breath", which, in turn, was her cue to counter-counter with, "Guess who's wanking tonight?" Strangely, I knew the answer to that one.

I've been a beer drinker most of my life. It's a family thing. My younger brother, who used to write a column on beer for *The Star*, was thinking about offering himself as a human shield to protect the first place where brewing took place in ancient Persia or, as it is known now, Iraq. But he took into consideration the fact that Dubya Bush is something of a Christian fundamentalist, and a reformed alcoholic to boot, and, possibly thinking beer is a weapon of mass destruction, might aim straight at him.

While beer is not something I would die for, I swear by it as the drink of choice when looking for the perfect woman. It's safe because it doesn't give too much away about you. It looks manly, a thirst quencher rather than a blatant method of inebriation. No woman will walk into a bar, see a man sipping on a beer and think to herself: "Hmmm, an accountant has walked in off the street and seems to be stuck to the bar. I shall ask the barman to fetch the fly spray."

No, go for a beer and drink a beer you like, not a beer you think is cool because you have been turned by the advertisements. When you walk up the bar, have in mind the beer that you would like and do not ask a barkeep "What beer do you have?" This is the equivalent of asking a chemist what flavour condoms he has. It is embarrassing to both you and the fellow behind the counter. Keep it simple, ask for your beer and, should they not have it, pause for a second, then give him your second choice in a calm voice. For the love of God, try make sure that your second choice is of the same type as the first. If you ask for a certain pilsner and it is not in stock, then ask for a second pilsner. Do not be a beer snob and react in horror should your first choice not be available. I have too many friends who make a song and dance about the type of beer they drink, when, in truth, they couldn't tell one from the other in a blind tasting. I order my beer according to the mood I'm in, the weather or, even, the food I eat. Pilsner is good with fish and chicken, lager is perfect after a game of football and you can't beat a Guinness or a pint of Boddington's on a cold winter's day. Make sure you know your drinks and can explain why you drink them when asked. Do not just say that you enjoy it. When the perfect woman asks, be ready with a story about your beer; it's as good an opening gambit as any.

An example:

I have a liking for Pilsner Urquell, the Czech beer. Now, this was the first golden beer brewed in the world. Before that, beers were cloudy, but in the Bohemian town of Pilsen they air-dried their malt instead of roasting it, which produced a clear beer that you could see through, plus they had very soft water in Pilsen. It revolutionised the beer industry, with glass becoming a preferred container for drinking… Er, hang on, maybe don't get carried away as I do when talking about beer. It might be best to stick with a short, romantic story about the brewer smuggling a closely guarded strain of hop out of Bavaria that gives the beer its hoppy taste and leave it at that. Spend too much time talking beer and the girl will start backing away slowly, keeping her eye on you.

Dave Faries, who writes a column about drinking for the *Dallas Observer*, asked himself the all-consuming question: "What does your drink say about you?" He, an impressive drinker in his own right, spent a goodly amount of time researching the topic and found that "gender, environment, and colour all influence a drink's meaning". From a friend, a whisky drinker, he gleaned the notion that someone who prefers clear drinks like vodka "is a serious drinker, someone who's not fucking around". And a bartender at a place called the Martini Ranch reckoned that "a drink probably says more about who the person wants to be", but that gin drinkers are usually people who just want to get a buzz on.

"We allow women greater latitude than men when ordering in public," writes Faries. "For example, Shelley, who refused to reveal her last name, points out that if a man 'drinks something with an umbrella in it, he's either a bit dodgy or extremely confident'. Certain drinks that are taboo for men – white wine, fruit drinks – are a staple for women; yet traditionally male drinks, such as whisky, simply enhance a woman's image. Ah, the pitfalls of drinking. Attempt to fit in, and you risk being shunned. Stand out, and the risks – and rewards – double. It's a fine line, really. Ultimately, however, when someone orders a bland beer or a trendy drink (such as a cosmopolitan), it expresses a mere desire to blend into the crowd. On the other hand, informed drinkers of whatever distinction, beer, wine, or even boat drinks, earn immediate respect."

Faries has a solid list of guidelines:

Clear drinks: The drinker is hell-bent on killing a few brain cells and doesn't care if you come along for the ride or not.

Brown drinks: reflect an educated lush, unless the bottle says "Jim Beam".

Domestic beer: one of the crowd, a nobody.

Imported beer: an educated drinker, or a foreigner.

White wine: see umbrella drinks

Umbrella drinks: suitable only for women. Otherwise, don't ask, don't tell.

A man drinking a cosmo is a man wearing pink panties.

WHERE TO DRINK

Perhaps one of the greatest evils of the last two centuries has been the franchise pub. Theme bars have sprouted like poisonous mushrooms around the world, closing down the small pub and, thus, the "local". There's one around every corner, so the advertising goes, and they will make you feel at home with the same pies, the same beers, the same look to every damn pub. It's an indictment of the laziness of modern society that this is so, but it is what we seekers of the perfect woman have been burdened with and we must make the best of it.

These may be the memories that we will keep of our first meeting with the perfect woman, the basis for the stories we will tell when our grandchildren gather around our feet at Christmas and ask: "Where did you meet Grandma, Granddad?" "Well, you couldn't miss her, my boy. She was standing at the far end of the local branch of the Two Dogs bar. The light from the fluorescent Urquell sign was shining off her eyes as she stood there with her two skank friends…" "Why was it called Two Dogs, Gramps?" "Well, there were these two dogs and they really liked each other… "

There are still bars out there that have managed to resist the lure of the franchise shilling, but they are few and far between. If you find them, treat them with respect and only

85

tell your loved ones about them, for they are the perfect women of the drinking world and you don't want everyone to find out.

Irish Theme Bars

Having been born in Northern Ireland and having lived there until I was ten, I have never worked out the attraction of the Irish theme pub. Perhaps I wasn't looking carefully enough when I went back to the country of my birth for a post-university visit but, when I frequented its bars, I couldn't see a single fucking goat's head on the wall, nor the fucking coats of arms of the four provinces of Ireland, nor a bunch of waiters dressed in fucking green waistcoats. I have been into proper Irish bars in the village my mother was born in and they are small, smoky places in which people swear and blaspheme often and loudly, and often break the law by staying open after the official closing time. This is called a lock-in and, should the police arrive, it could also be a lock-up for the proprietors.

I don't ever recall seeing a perfect woman in any of the proper Irish bars, which is a good thing, as the way my cousins had me drinking I wouldn't have been able to speak to them without embarrassing myself. Back in South Africa, however, the Irish theme bar is an acceptable place to go to, and I have been dragged along there by well-meaning but misguided friends, who do not understand my loathing of these places. The women who go there, however, are a varied and impressive lot with good teeth and impressive capacities for alcohol. Tread carefully.

Chill Bars

Why are chill bars always so hot? Not hot as in cool, but hot as in hot, damn hot. The places are stationary lifts, elevators that go nowhere, playing elevator music and serving drinks to numb your mind to the seamless trip-hop and dumbed-down drum 'n' bass. Yet, cool chicks go to chill bars; hot birds are in abundance. Check out Camps Bay if you don't believe me. The girls are, however, usually pretty young or, as I prefer to look at it, perfect women in training.

These are not places for serious drinkers, but for serious small-talkers, with the emphasis on small. In chill bars you will nod your head a lot and agree that everything is indeed cool, all the while looking as though you have been on the most amazing drug rush. It's easy to pretend you have taken drugs, simply say "hey" often, hood your eyes and let your head flop back slightly. If anyone asks you what you coming down from, just smile and say nowt. They'll think you're, well, cool.

Cocktail Lounges

If secretaries and desperate housewives are your definition of the perfect woman, then the cocktail lounge is the perfect place. Women drink cocktails because they don't taste of booze, which kinda defeats the purpose, doesn't it? No-one lounges in cocktail lounges, but they do, with the rush of five happy-hour strawberry daiquiris in them, lunge at men. Perhaps that's what we should call being pounced upon by a drunk woman: the cocktail lunge. We could get David Attenborough to do a programme on the mating ritual of the double-breasted pisshead: "Here we are," he would say breathlessly, as is his way, "in the animal's natural habitat.

Look at how her chest heaves as she approaches her prey, a little unsteady on her pins, her mascara a little wonky, but sure of her intentions and, in the words of the skank tribe, absolutely gagging for it. Her prey is leaning back against the bar, having become inadvertently separated from his pack, his instincts telling him that someone's on to him…" Cocktail bars? If you're looking for your perfect woman, never trust a drink that comes in a glass with sharp angles, has crushed ice or a sexual innuendo for a name. It might help you get laid, though.

Cigar Lounges

As I don't smoke, I don't really get cigar lounges, and your chances of meeting women here are slim. Yet, women love the image of men with cigars. Cigar bars are show-off places for rich men and women. A friend of mine who earns a pretty penny himself and hates smokers, said he wanted to teach himself to smoke cigars so he would look monied. Sharon Krum, on cigarlife.com, writes that women hit cigar bars because that's where the men are. "That's where the new mating dance is being danced, step by sexy step," she claims. Women once pretended to like sports to get our attention, she continues, and now its cigars, making cigar bars the new singles bar, "for a certain kind of single, with a certain amount of disposable income". Believe that if you like – she's writing for a cigar website, after all – and if you have disposable income, then perhaps this is your place. But a word of worry: your breath will smell almost as bad as the woman's.

Sports Bars

I have met women in sports bars, and have even had a date in one. She said she was a sports nut, I had a spare Saturday off and thought it would be a good idea to watch a rugby match with her. As a rule, I don't wear replica sports kit, unless it belongs to the mighty Liverpool Football Club, even though I am given loads by sponsors. But on this occasion I wore a Springbok jersey and brought one along for her to wear. It was sweet, I thought, and so did she. What wasn't sweet were the questions, which started at the first whistle and didn't stop until an hour after the Springboks had lost again (this was a couple of years ago when we lost *a lot*). "Did we win the toss?" Yes. "Why did he knock the ball on?" Because he's a prick. "What is the referee saying to him?" Some nonsense. "Why is the ball oval?" Because a woman designed it…

I guess what I'm trying to say is that you're not going to pick up your perfect woman in a sports bar.

CLOSING TIME

Bars will play an important role in your search for the perfect woman. As you will see, as you head through this book, they are a constant theme in my personal quest. You need to fuel your journey with something and booze is as good a flammable substance as any. Bars and pubs will be your friends through the good times and the dark times. Use them well.

3

MISS ROBOTO. THE SEDUCTIVE ART OF MODERN TECHNOLOGY

or the interminably shy, of whom, I think I have already mentioned, I am one, cyberspace has been both saviour and a curse in the search for the perfect woman. It is a public hidey hole from which to converse with members of the opposite sex without having to drag yourself through the excruciating blush of hoping to meet someone through accident or design in real life.

A friend of mine told me that cyberspace was a "smorgasbord of chicks", but I've never seen the connection between women and food, nor love, affection or even sex and food for that matter. I have, hand on my heart, never called a woman "honey", nor "cookie", "pumpkin pie" or "sugar-puff". Love and women are not edible; they are as hard to digest as seven pints of Guinness and a roasted knuckle of pig, and cause twice as much heartburn and anguish. No, food should not be used to describe the wonder of women because it is an insult both to them and to the beautiful bounty that is on our table today, for which we give thanks to our respective deities. Women and food are different because no-one says grace before they bed a woman, kneeling with the beloved one (or soon to be loved one) at the side of the bed and thanking the Lord for what they are about to receive. (Though a friend once told me the story of how he convinced a women to grace him with oral sex in his car, which was parked near a cathedral. As she pulled his member out, he told her, "For what you are about to eat, may the Lord make you truly thankful." She was, luckily for him, a dimwitted girl, who thought this very funny and carried on unperturbed.)

No, the food analogy simply does not work when applied to women and the sex we all pray to have with them. Why, for instance, are women a "smorgasbord", which implies a variety of the finest foods, most of which are probably not good for us? Why can't women be a cheese board or a breakfast buffet? Why must they always be delicacies or desserts or condiments? It makes them sound bad for us, full-fat globules that clog our arteries, make us obese and chase us to an early grave. Why don't we name women after healthy foods or even booze, both of which we should consume in equal quantities to ensure a long but happy life.

(A friend of mine, cricket journalist Neil Manthorpe, wrote a book called *The Beer Drinker's Guide to Losing Weight* some years ago. I was bought two copies of it for Christmas of 1997. It's a fine and honourable book, which has sound principles, some of which I use. Point being that Manners is still quite thin and manages to knock away his fair share of grog so he must have known what he was talking about.) Surely, wheatgrass, that wonder vegetable that has all the nutrition of a day's worth of veggies in one shot glass, deserves its place on the list of pet names? Then there's oat porridge, baked beans, Parmesan, Camembert, milk stout, port, skinless chicken breast, beef fillets…

Choose your favourite snack or bowel mover, and use it the next time someone inflicts a pet name upon you:

"How are you today, honey?"

"Spiffing, my high-fibre-bran-with-extra-dates-and-other-gut-ripping-items muffin."

"You sweet today, pumpkin?"

"Yes, you little single malt, you."

"Morning, sugar."

"G'day, crispy back bacon with waffle syrup."

Food and women do not go together, unless it's the two of you over dinner. In the era of the reality show, using foods as pet names is a dangerous occupation, which will snowball on to television in a flash. Calling someone pumpkin pie (what the hell is pumpkin pie anyway?) could lead to the BBC commissioning a programme called "You are who you eat", which will take in the sex lives of men and women who have a penchant for oral sex. It will investigate how going down on someone changes the lives and physical appearances of the people involved and what sort of people you should be performing oral sex on… er, I think I should stop right there. You know what I mean.

Bugger, I've got carried away again. Food and sex tend to do that to me, and don't get me started on beer again, although as I write this I am sitting in a hotel in Melbourne watching a very fine advertisement for Tooheys New lager, in which they catapult hops, barley and two women into a cloud so that it will rain beer. It may be a dream, but it's as good a dream as I'll have today.

Where was I? Hmmm, yes, cyberspace or, more broadly, technology has both broadened and narrowed the search for the perfect woman. Handheld computers have replaced holding hands, hands-free phones have taken over from hands-free sex, we can peruse endless shop windows full of available women and can push a women to orgasm with the use of a keyboard and throbbing, hard, telephone line.

It's worse than heroin, man. It's addictive, man, how is it addictive. It sucks you in because it gives you a sense of being involved and yet safe at the same time, delivering the rush without the incredible cost, messy run-ins with the law and rehabilitation involved with taking your usual class As. Some get so addicted to internet dating that it becomes their only world, instead of what it is meant for: a conduit to meeting others. Used thus, it is merely running to stand still and defeats the purpose of the search for the perfect woman. One can easily fritter away hours and hours contemplating the navel of others without actually getting to see one in real life. Let me tell you this for free: I have seen navels in real life, indeed, I have seen them in bright daylight and touched them under the cover of darkness, and I can tell you that they are well worth the contemplating in person.

For you, the modern man, this is an important chapter, for it will outline the good and evil of the technology available to us. It may even teach some of you how to use it properly, avoiding the trap of becoming an addict, like that guy in *Trainspotting* who lost his girlfriend and asked Ewan McGregor to get him some heroin so he could try it just once. He died a horrible and shitty death. Not that I am saying this will happen to you, but there is every danger that, should you get hooked, you will end up trapped in front of your computers and glued to your mobile telephones for the rest of your lives. You will think you are looking for the perfect woman, but you are not. You are avoiding it, putting off the inevitable moment when you one day have to meet up in person. You will lie to your friends and family about what you've been up to, making up extra-mural activities to hide the endless hours you are logged on. You will reason to yourself: "Just one more datingbuzz.com subscription and I'll get myself clean."

Trust me on this. I was/am such a person and still get the twitches when I switch on a laptop.

TEXTUAL RELATIONS

SMSing and its influence on modern sexual relationships

The opposable thumb has evolved. Once it helped our

prehistoric ancestors to use rudimentary tools; now it is the digit responsible for social intercourse. It has learnt to move from holding a club and beating a mate into submission, to flicking across the keypad of a mobile telephone or a Blackberry with the speed and dexterity to suggest to her that you would like to get all submissive with her. It has taken non-verbal communication on to a new plane, lifted it to the point where it has replaced the need for vocal cords, grammar and facial expressions.

Is this a good thing? Of course not, but the proliferation of SMS or text, as it is known in some countries, has been such that to ignore it or not learn how to use it in the proper manner would be foolish. In China alone, mobile phone users sent almost 12 billion messages over the Spring holiday festival, which takes place over a week. The Chinese Ministry of Information Industry estimates that the Chinese sent 25 billion SMSes a month in 2005. That's 300 billion a year. To give an indication of the growth of text in China, about 1 billion messages were thumbed out in 2000. Someone's making a lot of money out of this.

In Jamshedpur, India, girls, banned by their parents from hooking up with their boyfriends, have been using cellphones and disguises to get around so that no-one can see them. In a land where dating is frowned upon, Hindu and Christian girls have been renting burqas, the traditional Muslim dress and, hidden behind the veil, have been texting their boyfriends to tell them where to meet them. In India, the new technological centre of the world, the SMS has invaded the popular psyche so well that it has inspired a song, written by pop star Remo Fernandes called *Love on SMS*. According to an Indian newspaper, Remo, who is 52 and a "love master", helps a shy, young lad pull a bird by giving him a cellphone and telling him that "SMS is the way to do it". It is not known whether Remo is actually sponsored by a cellphone provider, but you would suspect so.

In Britain, a survey of computer and mobile phone users found that they had used their cellphones to make the first step when meeting potential partners. One in five had had the courage to send a flirtatious message that led to a date and the good things that come after dating.

In the United States, the *San Francisco Chronicle* recently reported, the cellphone has been combined with internet dating services and is a market with massive potential. One of the newest fads is number plate dating. You're driving along and see someone you like. You type their number plate into your phone and, if they have registered their number plate details with a service provider, you can message the person there and then. Mini versions of online dating services can be browsed on cellphones and contact can be made via SMS. According to a website that is focused solely on SMSes, smallplanet.net has devised a system that will give you a Bluetooth alert on your phone if you are actually within speaking distance of someone who is compatible. Whether this is so you can actually talk to the person and see what they look like in real life, or run away in case they see you and want to engage in conversation, is, of course, entirely up to you. Other systems will do searches of cellphones in the immediate vicinity, say in a bar, and match the phones to profiles in the database. If they find someone that you fancy or who is a good match for you, they will tell you she is there and send you a picture of her so you can pick her out. As Hunter Heaney, the CE of smallplanet.net says: "It's about getting past that point of pain of going up to talk to someone at a bar."

The world is moving apace. I only learnt to use text messages late in life, but have caught up in a calloused rush. I could SMS for my country now and have had some success with it as a sexual tool, so to, er, speak. One Australian girl of my acquaintance told me that I was a "gorgeous" SMSer, which alerted me to the fact she had been trying to catch my eye for the week she had been of my acquaintance and told me that she wanted to get better acquainted. Being called a gorgeous anything will do that to me, except, as I have pointed out, being called a gorgeous pumpkin. It's not that I don't like pumpkin, it's… no, no, we've been down this road before. Don't get me started on food again.

When I received my first ever text I thought my phone was broken because it went beep and then stopped. I didn't know my phone could SMS and tentatively touched the green button to find it was from my then girlfriend – who was a clever clogs with technology – to tell me that she missed me and hoped to see me soon. So, for me, love and the SMS have been bedfellows since that first magical beep on my Nokia. I still get a chill when my phone vibrates in my pocket and sings to me. It's the same thrill that letters and phone calls gave me when I was younger.

At university I had a long-distance relationship with a girl back home. These were the days before email and cellphones. She used to send me letters, a couple each week, which spoke of how she missed me and day to day nonsense. If she called the residence and I was not there, the taker of the message would leave her name on the chalk board, asking me to call her. Every day I would check the board to see if she had called or if there was a letter with the legend "S.W.A.K." on the seal. It's that same buzz that the SMS brings, except that the SMS delivers it more often and wherever you are. Strangely, though, it does not seem to lessen the anticipation and the glee of the receiving.

Safe Text Etiquette

Just as there are rules for bars, so there are rules for SMSes because, if not watched over, they can get away from you like a nuclear reaction. Like letters, you can never take a text back and in some cases they can be used as evidence against you. Two larrikins I know have had to get divorced because their wives found incriminating evidence on their cellphones from their bits on the side. I make no apologies for them, I have no truck with people who cheat on others, unless there are extenuating circumstances (and one of them has a vague excuse that stands tall over a beer, but flops under the examination of a divorce lawyer). Both of them deserved all they got, a fact they will freely admit. Both of them, though, are now extremely wary of how they use their mobile phones and where they leave them. Dynamite comes in small electronic devices.

Do not drink and text

This is the first and the most important of all the rules. It is exactly like drinking and driving: you think you can get away with it, but inevitably you will crash or get pulled over by the cops and have to explain what possessed you to get behind the wheel. You should never get behind the keyboard when you've tucked a good few under your belt. Letting your fingers do the walking over those brightly coloured numbers when pissed will cause you great embarrassment in the morning when you wake up to find an SMS from your now ex-girlfriend asking what you meant when you said you wanted to still like her despite her new hair colour and funny-shaped nipples.

When you are drunk, you become a poet with a cellphone, your thumb a loquacious quill with which you believe you can convince that girl who has been playing hard to get, or whom you have been too afraid to approach, that you are the very man for her. You never say what you mean: "Let me compare thee to a summer's day" will end up as, "I tink your sweat." As sweet a demeanour as she may have, unless she really, really likes you, she will take it that you have demeaned her by sending an SMS when bombed. Tripping over your tongue and mangling your words when you are speaking face to face over some drinks is one thing, but, as I mentioned before, the SMS will remain in her cellphone's large memory for her to bring up at some time in the future. This will happen when she is drunk and it will not be pretty.

For many of us, writing is difficult enough an exercise when you are sober. I try to remain in some state of sobriety when I am writing, although much of this book has been, er, supplemented by the odd glass or bottle of something or other. Like driving a car, there is a limit to how many you can have before you are classed as unable to write. Unlike driving a car, there is no legal limit, no breathalysers can tell you if you should not be allowed to hit MENU and then scroll through to MESSAGE and then, like a blind man approaching an elephant trap, onwards to the sharp, poison-tipped spikes of the CREATE NEW MESSAGE. You will have to find your own level of acceptable SMS soberness through trial and error. For instance, some of the chapters of this book have been written under the influence of what I would like to call the six-beer advantage (some would say handicap, but they do not understand the lubricating and creative powers of the bottle); others have flowed over the Berlin Wall of writer's block thanks to the dryness a bottle of Sauvignon Blanc gave my addled wit, and not to mention the odd whisky.

A good indication of when not to SMS is when you feel an incredible urge to do so. If you think you need to SMS, you really, really shouldn't. If you are in a bar with your friends and having a good time, then why would you need to send a missive to the new miss unless you were going to do something daft. You are never hit by inspiration when you are sober and alone. Why would the spirit take you except because the spirits had already taken over your brain functions and turned you into the stud your mind has always known you were?

Some of the wrong things you will do when texting pissed include: the inappropriate use of four-letter words; direct requests for sex; using the "love" word; misspelling words, which gives away that you are drunk; mentioning how you would love to see bits of your target's anatomy naked and telling her, in graphic detail, exactly what those bits are and what you have fantasised doing to them; and, worst of all, breaking up.

Send to the right person

Pretty obvious this, isn't it? But when you hit send, please, please, please, make sure that it's to the one you mean it to be for. The lottery of sending to the miss wrong instead of miss right is too ghastly to contemplate and herewith a few stories of horror and woe.

I attended a launch of a golf tournament at a resort known for its hedonism. It is a place I have visited often and at which I have something of a reputation for thoroughly misbehaving myself. The official launch, an annual do that has become legendary amongst sports journalists, was an absolute ripper and the after-party was even better. The booze flowed so freely that talk, as it does amongst the bored, underworked and drunk, turned to sex and just how casual it could be made. Like Billy Connolly I have never believed that there can ever be such a thing as casual sex. Sex is anxious and frantic, your body assumes funny positions and the blood flows into areas it would have no business going near when you are at your most casual. This is not to be confused with causal sex, which is the logical procession of the mating dance – smiling, introducing, drinking, flirting, blushing, swapping of hotel room numbers, fumbling, tumbling, bumbling, the opening of small foil packets, rolling, prodding, apologising, a helping hand, inserting, thrusting, apologising again (guys, a useful Wilde quote for when this happens: "To be premature is to be perfect"), withdrawing, smoking, thinking, chatting, snoring and, then leaving and never calling again. Except for a drunk SMS late one night.

Casual sex only exists in theory, argued Connolly. Can you read a book while you're having a shag, chat about what you did at work when you're on the job, and be reminded that it's bin day tomorrow mid-bonk? No you cannot, and I used this argument during the post-launch party, much to the amusement of one of the prettier of the PR girls, on whom I had had my eye for some time. She laughed, touched me on the knee and made eye contact. Even then I wasn't entirely sure that she liked me until I offered to go to the bar to get the next round, and she offered to go with me. She must like me, I thought. When she offered to pay, I thought that she must like me a lot, but she told me it was on the company. I was confused, but having numbed my shyness into submission and wishing to get on the company if the company was her, I wooed her and was on the point of inviting her back to my room when she said she absolutely had to go to bed because she had to be bright-eyed and bushy-tailed in the morning.

I sulked and headed off to bed by myself. As I got to my room, I committed the sin of sins and sent her an SMS, telling her how "hot" I thought she was, what my room number was and how much I would appreciate it if she paid me a visit. I hit send by searching for her name and then fell asleep on top of my bed, fully clothed. She never arrived and I woke up sulky and went to breakfast. Halfway through my cheese omelette, my phone beeped. Ah, had my love answered me. Nope, but my ex-girlfriend's father, who liked me very much, had, thanking me for my "kind" message at 4am, but he was sorry he couldn't make it.

Check to whom you send your SMSes to. It will save you strife.

English as she is spoke
There is a website that translates SMS talk into proper English. It is called lingo2word.com and is the modern day dictionary for the post-literate generation. There are young men and women today for whom the English language is a series of substituted numbers and symbols, with grammar

thrown out the window. SMSes with poor grammar are just not sexy; the same goes for messages that use "2" and "4" in place of "to" and "for", as well as abbreviations.

For instance:
"Let me count the way I love thee" becomes "Let me count D wAz I lov thee". "

"You have the most delicious of smiles" transforms to "uv D most :-9 of *grins*".

"When the moon hits your eye like a big pizza pie, that's amore" is bastardised into "wen D m%n hits ur eye lk a big <) pie, dats amore".

Not very sexy, is it? Not at all. You'd have to be pig stupid to be turned on by that. The post-literate generation have Paris Hilton for their poster child, a celebrity with less substance than usual, who is famous because she is a rich heiress, has learnt how to pout and, on the evidence of the movie *One Night in Paris*, gives a mean blow job. Sex for the post-literates is a short, sharp jab to the nether regions with no heart, full of more "umf" than "oomph". Love written as luv? It just doesn't sound right, does it?

Use capital letters, use punctuation, read books, learn phrases, steal beautiful lines from those who get paid to write beautiful lines and use them in your messages so that you sound beautiful. Sending an SMS creates a fantasy of you in the receiver's mind, and you do not want that image to be of someone who thinks that a grin has an asterisk on either side of it, that a smile is a colon, a dash and a right bracket, and that they wink by using a semi-colon. Anyone who winks using a semi could well be someone who wanks using a semi, which is exactly the sort of response child-like text messages should stir in your loins.

Be original

A friend told me a version of this story some years ago and I thought it funny, if an urban legend. He attributed it to his friend, but I was devastated to find out that a player from the football club I love above all else (I have not yet met the perfect woman, remember) was the one actually responsible for it.

John Arne Riise, the Norwegian who patrols the left flank for the mighty Liverpool, was bust sending the same SMS to more than one woman in the hope that it would trigger stirrings in one of their loins. Norway has, I was surprised to discover, a quite active tabloid press, the hounds of which discovered he had hit "forward" on his cellphone and sent on the same chat-up line to "a range of well-known women". "Riise, who is a fixture with Champions League winners Liverpool, refused to comment after the newspaper *VG* unfurled the details of the 24-year-old's telephone seduction technique," it was reported. "*VG* revealed the names of at least ten celebrity women – singers, models and media personalities – who received the same flattering, if poorly written, message inviting them to a romantic dinner for two."

Badly-written? A football player, who would have thought? Well, at least they knew it was written by him. What the paper doesn't say is how many of those celebrity women fell for his scatter-gun SMS and went out on a romantic dinner for two or, if he was lucky enough, for three. His dream left foot, massive weekly salary and celebrity status are attractive enough attributes, and there are some who would overlook being part of a spam SMS to date Riise. Perhaps they are all Liverpool fans. If he helps Liverpool win the Premiership one year, I will date him myself.

Do not leave your phone unattended
Cellphone pranks are still all the rage with my friends. I have had the language on my phone changed to Samoan and, so I could no doubt SMS Riise, Norwegian, which necessitates a trip to the phone's manual to put it right. They also like finding out the number of the biggest girl in the bar and re-routing my phone calls to her phone so she thinks I am interested in her and people are calling her by mistake. Worst of all, though, they pick up your phone when you have disappeared to the bog and use it to send out SMSes – suggestive and seductive SMSes – to those girls you have been meaning to erase from your phone's memory, but never got around to deleting.

Keep your cellphone with you at all times or you, too, will be woken up late at night by Big Betty thanking you for getting in touch with her again, that she understands how you feel because she had the same feelings and she forgives you for running out of her flat at three in the morning and she knows you didn't do it because you were going to use her as a one-night stand and that you wanted more from her and now she is willing to give it you because of the sweet SMSes you sent her saying that you didn't think she was as big and as fat and as skanky as all the other boys thought she was. No, you don't want that to happen.

If you leave your phone on the table or out of reach, then

the perfect woman may just pick it up and be tempted to have a look through your messages. Unless you are an unsentimental being, you will keep old love messages the way that you keep old love letters. We all want to be loved and so we save those memories of the ghosts of lovers past. Should they be discovered, you will have some difficult questions to answer.

INTERNET DATING

There are a lot of liars on online dating sites. I know this because I crossed my fingers when filling in my profile, sucking in a tummy here when filling in "body type" and standing on tippy-toes for the "height" category. The internet is a veritable *Nip/Tuck* show, a cyberspace surgery for imaginary liposuction, face lifts and hair implants. There's nothing wrong with a bit of exaggeration, but there have been a lot of disappointed internet daters turning up for a date wearing a red rose and expecting to meet Brad Pitt, to find that he had got a lot shorter and put on a lot of weight since he hooked up with Angelina Jolie.

Yet, the online dating service has been one of the great success stories of the internet, a financial boom that shows little sign of hitting its plateau. It has been the subject of a study by three economists, Günter J Hitsch and Ali Hortaçsu from the University of Chicago, and Dan Ariely of the Massachusetts Institute of Technology, who applied an empirical study to one dating service. In their paper *What Makes You Click* they discovered that we are as fickle as ever, and want looks and money above all else. Most people rated their looks as being above average and yet never included a picture with their profile. The stereotypes held true: women wanted their potential partners to earn more than them; men were still wary of a woman with more bucks than them. Yet they finally hooked up with someone who looked like them.

I did not go on to the net searching for someone who looked like me – that would be daft. I wanted someone who looked a lot better than me so that if we decided to have children one day, then they could have her looks and my brains, or maybe even my feet, except for the little toe, which is a little crooked. Why narrow the gene pool by mating with your equal, I thought, aim above yourself, give the planet a chance to better itself, while at the same time, showing off with a good-looking bird on your arm.

On the net you can specify your perfect woman, down to the smallest detail. It is an online supermarket of perfect women. From hair and eye colour to height, weight and whether she is with child or without. Fancy an instant family without the late nights and the smell of baby puke? Click on the babe with the four-year-old. Looking for a cheerleader who can cook and thinks that home is where the heart is? Hit the left button on your mouse and she might just be yours.

The owners of the dating websites, who, let's be honest, like putting punters' money in their pockets that little bit more than they like putting people together, have not yet divided their sites into supermarket aisles. Redheads and ginger nuts in aisle number one, platinum, golden and dirty blondes in aisle number two, skanks next to the fast food section and businesswomen looking for a soulmate in frozen foods. Perhaps in a few years they will put a sell-by and use-by date on profiles and charge less for the viewing of those profiles that are closer to spoiling than the fresher young seasonal fruits who have signed on.

The Times of London investigated the phenomenon and discovered that sites have indeed become more and more specific. They tell the tale of a woman called Louise who loved her horse, an Irish gelding called Tigs, so much that she not only enjoys riding a horse that was castrated to keep him in his place, but she refuses to be without him and wants the new man in her life to accept this. Unfortunately men who like coming second to an Irishman with no willy are few and far between, but then Louise discovered a website just for her: LoveHorse.co.uk. She found a 33-year-old cattle farmer who was looking for a riding partner and soulmate, moved Tigs to his farm and they are now living together. Along the way, Louise also came across some weirdos. One fella, called "Whippy", was "a submissive male slave looking for a bossy/dominant horsey male/female". The picture he posted showed him wearing only boots and jodhpurs, and brandishing the whip he apparently wanted used on him. Louise said neigh to his advances.

The Times also found that there were other very specific sites. LoveAir.co.uk was full of cabin crew members looking for love, a strange thing for a group who by all accounts get their jollies during flight stopovers in countries or cities far away from home. There is also LoveYoga.com for the flexible and seekers of karma amongst you. As mentioned earlier, I did find a site called perfectwoman.com, but it was for breast enhancement products, while the plural, perfectwomen.

com is a portal to a group of porn sites that bombarded my laptop with so many, er, pop-ups that I almost went blind trying to close them all. A splash of stolen holy water on the keyboard and they disappeared in a puff of smoke.

Internet dating has not taken over totally. Research shows that just over ten per cent of singles in Europe have used or even just browsed online dating, which means that 90 per cent are using the more traditional methods of hanging around bars or being set up by friends. Site owners are excited by the potential growth that dragging that 90 per cent out there to the computer screens will bring, and are quite happy that modern life is making more and more men and women reclusive. The focus on careers has given us little time to hunt and gather mates and, with the net enabling us to do the hunting during working hours, more of us are staying indoors to find someone to stay indoors with.

Why are you online?

Judging by the summaries slapped onto their websites, no-one really seems to know why they go on to an online dating site. Some try to blame others, saying that they are there because their friends and family either told them to be there or signed them up without their knowing. That's all very American of them, shifting the blame, putting their lives in the hands of others. People like that shouldn't be allowed to be on dating sites. They will not turn out to be good dates because they are looking for someone to give direction to their lives, and will later turn on that person because they don't like the direction that it's going in. Do not hang around these people. Simply point them towards the setting sun, explain to them that what they seek is on the horizon and sinking fast and push them off towards it in a rickety boat.

Indeed, it shows the shift in attitude towards internet dating that so many people are apparently encouraging other to get jiggy with it online, or so I thought until I saw an incentive scheme offering free extensions to subscriptions for every friend you sign up. It's like knowing someone who has just got into selling life insurance and feels nothing about tapping up his friends for a buck or two for policies they don't really need.

Others get online because they have recently ended a marriage and are trying to meet people outside their husbands' groups of friends. Some do it because they have moved cities and want to sneak into a social circle, some do it for sex, some for kinky sex, some because they are approaching 30 and are under pressure to get married, and most of them because they are just a little bit more lonely than they think they really ought to be.

I would like to tell you that I joined a dating site only for research purposes for this book, but I have been scanning singles sites for a while. When I joined I was asked by more than one woman why I was there. I told them that I was writing a book on the subject of looking for a perfect woman and thought this was as good a place as any to find one. All of them were sceptical and asked me if research was the only reason and I agreed it wasn't. There's a lonely person in all of us. I was there because I knew the perfect woman was out there somewhere. I just didn't know what she looked like or where she was.

The profile
I have always been insecure about sending my details out

over the internet. I am big-headed enough to think that somewhere in a darkened room in Langley is a computer that will go "bing" as soon as my details are downloaded on to the net. What if internet dating is just a front for the CIA and they are using sites to broaden their database and hunt down known dissidents? There were those anti-apartheid marches at university I went on, I knew the words to the Special AKA's "Free Nelson Mandela" and could toyi-toyi with the best of them. I missed at least two tutorials during student boycotts in protest against the university's administration, but that was because my politics lecturer told us all to get out and experience political activism on the street. I did, but got bored, and took my political activism down to the pub to drink a beer to toast the struggle's very good health.

Filling out the profile on a dating site is a tricky exercise. Be sure of one thing, you will tell lies. I started off fine:

Profile name: Kevmac (And just so I wouldn't attract the wrong person, I added "Beer and loafing" as a subhead.)
   Age: 38
   Star sign: Libra

Okay. So far so good. Ah, a tricky one…

Height: Well, I'm 1.70m, but what's 5cm between strangers… 1.75m
   Body type: The choices here are: "Ask me later"; "Slim"; "Athletic"; "Average"; "Curvaceous"… hang on, "curvaceous"? The site said they had offered this option for those who felt they fell in between average and the

next choice, "a few extra pounds". Then there was "large", "disabled" and "other". The last of those, presumably, is for prop forwards and survivors of Chernobyl. I hovered over "a few extra pounds" for a few minutes, then "average", before sucking in my tummy and treating myself to "athletic".

Looks: Ah, no problem here. "Very attractive." My mother told me so.

Hair colour: Black

Eye colour: Now, I don't really know what colour my eyes are. I was told once that they are brown, or hazel with green flecks in them. I once told a girlfriend, with whom I had been going out with for three weeks that I loved her green eyes. She told me they were blue. So, I went with "ask me later".

Cultural characteristics: Very PC this one... I'll stick with white-caucasian, although when I grow up I want to be a Pacific Islander.

Home language: English and, after enough to drink, Swahili, Cantonese and shorthand.

Religion: Retired Catholic

Education: Yes, but don't tell my university. A professor at my alma mater once wrote a letter to my newspaper slating me badly for a column I had written. He questioned my journalistic ethics. I refrained from replying to him, telling him that I had an honours degree from his department and had won a good couple of awards. But I am not a bitter person.

Profession: Writer/journalist

Income: Comfortable. My cheque account has airbags.

Relationship status: Single, you twit. It's supposed to be a singles site.

Relationship type sought: All of them, except ones related to me by blood.

Drinking habits: "I like the occasional drink". Another lie, as you may have worked out by this stage.

Smoking habits: I only smoke after sex. (No need to tell them I haven't smoked for years.)

Have children: My brother's two boys come around on a Saturday afternoon to tap me up for protection money. I give them ten bucks each and they promise to play outside and not to annoy me.

Want children: Hmmm... ask me later... like when you lose the urge to have children.

On the "More about me" section, you get to tell more half truths:

Hair style: Short

Facial hair: Clean-shaven (At least twice a week it is. I'm a cyclist and I shave my legs more than I shave my face.)

How's your eyesight? I wear cool glasses, but I don't have to, not really. It's just that I think they give me a certain academic air. Mostly, though, my glasses sit on top of my head because that looks cool as well. It says I am clever, but tough clever. I can put a four-letter word in front of a long, clever antique one. I'm a renegade writer, like the good Doc Hunter S Thompson, except that I don't have big guns, his controlled madness and I'm still alive. So, it doesn't mean that I am ashamed of my glasses when I eventually opt for: "ask me later".

Do you have any disabilities? Apart from those fucking spectacles (see, four-letter word and then a long, cleverish one), no.

What is your HIV status? Jesus, what a question… Negative.

Do you have any body art? No.

Fashion sense? No, but thanks for asking.

Favourite clothes: Shorts and T-shirt.

Personality traits: Daring, easy-going, funny, outgoing, naïve, outrageous, outspoken, shy. That about covers all bases, I reckon. The only one to leave out is moody. That is a woman's prerogative, and I shall not trespass there.

How would you describe your sense of humour? I'm on this site, aren't I?

How do friends rate your intelligence? A girl once said I was a genius, but that was because I used a coat hanger to open her car when she had locked her keys in it. There's no space for: Managed to get through university without failing a year despite scheduling lectures around football matches, happy hours and lunches down at the beach. That's pretty clever.

What rules you the most? I think Jupiter, but it could be Saturn.

At a party you'd call me? From the other side of the room even though I didn't mean to fart.

Then on to Leisure Activities…

How do you spend your free time? Surfing your bloody website (how many more questions are there?).

Your favourite types of music: Ones with notes, chords, bars and shit.

Do you enjoy reading? Only that wonderful new book on the market called *In Search of South Africa's Perfect Woman*. You really must buy a copy for yourself and your friends.

What television, movies, etc… Blah, blah, blah… it's all

getting a bit much now...

How much time do you spend at work? There was an option here I really liked: "What's work?"

What would be your dream home? Mine, when I get the pool fixed, the gutters mended and finish paying for the bastard.

Then we come to the narrative stage, where you tell a little bit more about yourself. Here you are allowed considerable leeway. Mine read thus and was honest to a point:

"Well, not quite beer and loafing. Some beer and a little loafing, although there are times when there is loathing, but that's usually just after a few beers when I've been watching the Boks play away from home.

"If that sounds like I'm a typical Seffrican boy because I love sport and beer, well I'm not. It's what I do. It's my job (er, sport, not beer, although I do have a rather close relationship with manufacturers of beer). I'm involved in the sports industry in this country.

"I travel a fair amount each year, depending on the job, both internationally and in South Africa. Live in Joburg, but love Cape Town. I love cycling and play football fairly regularly. Have just started a fitness programme... and have been going well for the last, um, lemme see, two days. Have a small beergut to rid myself of, but am lucky in that once I'm into the rhythm I lose weight quickly.

"Too much information? Yeah, quite possibly, but damn it all to buggery, you gotta walk the talk... no, hang on, you have to walk and talk and chew gum... no, no... ah, Christ, I give up..."

If describing yourself is walking a fine line, then defining the features of your perfect woman is tiptoeing on a razor blade. If you are a nice, accommodating chap, like me, you should widen your parameters just enough to remain seemingly nice and accommodating. It's a wide cast of the dating net that has pulled in a few beautiful fish, but snagged a few sharks and whales along the way.

My narrative for my ideal match ran thus:

"I've been told that I'm single because I'm too picky, but that's not right. It's because I'm far too shy for my own good (which is strange considering what I do for a living). Well, perhaps shy is too strong a word… bashful, may be better… no, that's not right either, Bashful was a dwarf.

"I'm looking for someone who likes to go on sushi binges, eating the stuff until we can no more: someone who will wake up with me in the morning and suggest a jolly good shag before we go to work/football/the pub (if not a jolly good one, then a jolly one at least); someone who would be cool with me suggesting that we find ourselves a proper pub or a wine bar on a Sunday, and sit down and talk the biggest load of bollocks for hours without getting bored; someone who isn't too precious; someone who will giggle/sigh/tickle during sex; someone who will giggle/sigh/tickle during chats; and someone who likes Blur a lot."

Yeah. That's witty, clever and with the right amount of sass. I sat back and waited for the women to come running … and I waited… and waited… then one landed or rather kicked the door down and told me that I should contact her because she was all woman. She was 45, curvaceous and wealthy and told me that we should chat because she was all woman and knew what she wanted. I couldn't reply because I had forgot to take out a subscription, but she took this as an insult and berated me:

"You'll never know what you have missed. One day you will hear a song on the radio and it will be me and you will not know it is me. I am, completely, all woman."

She must have really liked the cut of my jib, because she zoomed in on my profile on another site I had set up a profile on. When I did not succumb to her "I am all woman" routine, she called me a loser and headed off to stomp on some other poor bastard.

My mistake was in being too vague, my net was too wide and I began attracting fat white and black women aged 40 and up. I have nothing against fat white and black women aged 40 and over, but neither do I wish to hold anything attached to me against them either. A polite "Thanks for calling, I will contact you when I get a subscription" was enough of a barge pole to dissuade most of them. Some, flotsam on the sea of loneliness, grabbed on to the barge pole and held on for dear life. They are still there, I am ashamed to say, but I have not the heart to cast them adrift. I know how they feel. I am clinging on to a few barge poles myself, 68 barge poles at the last count. Wait, I've just seen another that I like and have added to my favourite list. Make that 69. Oh, look, another… 70 and counting…

High profile
On most dating websites you are asked to provide a user name, which will become your pet name, as well as a subhead, a one-line kicker that is something funny or deep.

Mine was "Beer and loafing", which pretty much speaks for itself.

The administrators of websites should, however, put a limit on how many women are allowed to put "What you see is what you get", after their names, because it does them no favours and, having fibbed on my own profile, I know that others are going to fib on theirs. What I see is not what I will get, and if it is, ladies, read carefully, and do not use these lines. Fight against the cliché, it will only do you good. Stupid men like clichés because they like the familiar and safe. They will not be the adventurous lovers you are hoping for.

"I know what I want and what I'm worth." Perhaps, but I bet I can talk you down to a decent price.

"Live each day as though it is your last." I do, and get in trouble for it often. If we got together I surely would live each day as if was my last and would end it wondering why my life hadn't ended.

"If you can't be good, be good at it." Hmmm…

"I am woman." Ah, thanks dear, I was wondering.

"I am woman, hear me roar." I am man, hear me bore.

"I am me." Therapy junkie.

"Who am I?" Therapy junkie with a drinking problem.

"If u snooze u loose." At least I didn't sleep through my English lessons.

"If a man speaks in a forest and no-one hears him, is he still wrong? *grin*" Only if you are the one not hearing him… grin…

"Life is not measured by the number of breaths you take, but by the moments that take your breath away." Has a problem with flatulence.

"Rock my world." 'Smoke on the waterrrrrr, fire in the sky!'

"Dance like no one is watching, sing like no one is listening, love like you've never been hurt." And drink like someone else is paying the bill.

There are original sinners on the internet, though, women who know how to twist a phrase and turn a man's head. The best I came across was from craigslist.com, where a woman had outlined over 50 reasons to like her.

I'm likely to have a different hair colour every time you see me.

I'm slippery when wet.

I'll make you laugh.

I'll pretend I didn't see you look at that chick with the big boobs.

I'll always be impressed with how strong you are.

I know that handcuffs aren't just for the cops.

I can dance.

I'll make fun of you.

I like porn.

I give road head.

I like it when you pull my hair.

I'll let you beat me at pool.

I like it when dogs sleep in the bed.

My heart will jump every time you walk through the door.

I'll think you're just about the coolest person I know.

I won't sleep with your friends.

The kinkier the better.

The only drama I have any part of is on television.

I can tie a cherry stem with my tongue.

My kisses will take your breath away.

I dig public sex.

I know a lot about movies.

I'd fuck Angelina Jolie too.

I'll thank you every time you open the door.

I'll never waste your love.

I'd never give you shit in front of your friends.

I don't need batteries.

I once ate a cricket.

I'll always have smooth legs.

I like it when my hair gets messed up.

My daughter already has a dad.

I like action movies.

I smell pretty good most of the time.

When I can, I give to charity.

I can be ready in 30 minutes or less.

I lose at arm wrestling every time.

I've got dirty pictures of me on my computer.

I'll look cute in your shirt.

I am old enough to remember when the space shuttle crashed.

I still get drunk.

I won't ever leave make-up on your shoulder.

I can balance a cheque book.

I'll never say 'nothing's wrong' when something is.

I have never stabbed anyone in the eye.

I can count to 100 by 5s.

I think it's hot when you masturbate.

I know that whipped cream goes on more than strawberries.

I know that objects in the mirror are bigger than they appear.

I may have already won the Lotto.

I never run with scissors.

I know how to keep a secret.

There are other approaches to take. A South African divorcée, who had been on and then left the website because she had not found anyone who "blew her hair back", returned with a vengeance and quite the best bit of narrative I have read on an online dating site:

"Single, hatchet-faced, white female in dead-end job seeks dumpy neurotic male for mutual psychological torture, tepid sex and co-dependency. I enjoy drinking, smoking, pornography and self-righteous indignation. I can't stand movies or music. I have middling intelligence but try to appear smarter by affecting a world-weary air, memorising useless facts and chuckling at my own mean-spirited, agenda-driven jokes.

"I'm 43, but look 53 and feel 63. My perfect night would include getting hammered in a sleazy bar while you flirt with seedy drunken women, followed by an embarrassing screaming match. I would be open to an unsatisfying fling that leaves me filled with regret and dread but prefer a long-term, soul-crushing descent into booze and pills.

"Oh. And I LOVE everything. Everything. From leaping out of hot air balloons to cavorting with Buddhist Monks."

I am not her type, she said, because I am too short, am not a long-haired artist and do not have a photograph. Ah, the photograph. The photograph is all important on websites. Even here beauty is as deep and as broad as your computer's screen. Women whose initial photographs show someone with blonde hair, a tan and a smile get the most hits. Those who combine this with a challenge, as one girl did, calling herself: Dare2FlipMeOver, and who put the numbers "69" after their names shoot up the most popular profiles rating of dating sites.

And even though www means WORLD-WIDE web, there are still those amongst us who think that the world is not a small place. I have come across pictures of Shania Twain posted on the profile of a woman who said that she was from Auckland, New Zealand. Jennifer Lopez is apparently so desperate for a third husband that she has moved to Cardiff, has become "curvaceous", loves rugby and can speak Gaelic as a second language. On an American-based website, two men thought that New Zealand was far enough away for them to use the same picture of All Black Richie McCaw. One of them worked in a Las Vegas casino, the other was a "law enforcer" from Boston.

A close friend met a man through the internet. They hooked up and within two weeks, much to the shock of her friends and parents, they were engaged. She showed me a photograph of him she had taken after they had spent a weekend together. He had a squashed face with too much skin, a nose with nostrils almost the same size as his mouth, and eyes that hid lies.

"I'm so relieved. He looks so much better than he did on the net," she told me. "What do you think?"

"Jesus, how bad did he look on the net?" I asked, and she never asked me again. A month later she called and told me that they had broken up. She had found out that he had been married twice before and was still going through a divorce. Oh, and he had a teenage daughter and his house was a lot smaller than he had promised. She had sold the ring, she said, and had bought a load of booze. Was I free to help her drink it?

There is a bit of the voyeur in all of us and there is a bit of the peep show in all online dating websites. Sometimes, I must admit, that when I am online and cruising I feel some of what Elvis Costello was singing about when he said he knew how it felt to be inside a pornographer's trousers. There's something not quite right about internet singles sites, but there is also something very necessary about them. They open up more avenues and lanes in the search for the perfect woman. Some have had success, but the numbers of others still surfing cyberspace tell another story, a tale of desperation that cannot be rectified in the cold darkness of the ether. In cyberspace, no one can hear you scream, but neither can they hear you dream.

4

THE DATING GAME

I do not date much, as you may have gathered from the earlier chapters of this book. During my teenage years I could probably count the number of dates I had on the palm – I mean, fingers – of one hand. Apart from my interminable shyness with girls when I was a kid, I also never liked going to movies much and I hated milkshakes. I thought it was a very American thing to do and, again, as you may have worked out, I'm not too crazy about the Americanisation of the planet. Plus, I am really, really bad at small talk. I do big talk pretty well, but talking twaddle with someone you don't really know? As someone once said of the Queen, who has to make small talk with all manner of her subjects over all manner of subjects, she's a patient chick, that one.

In her younger days the Queen would have made a good date. Liz was a bit of a looker when she was still a princess and, by that stage, was already a master of polite, nonsensical chatter.

"How do you do?"

"Wonderful, thank you, your majesty. And how do you do?"

"Splendid, thank you for asking. Enjoying the weather?"

And so on. Don't you wish that just once the Queen would wake up one day and think: "Right. I'm, like, the richest bird in Great Britain, plus that pesky Northern Ireland bit, although they do have good oysters and mussels and I do like a bit of Bushmills in my tea. I have my own boat, a huge bastard of a castle, 71 nations who consider themselves part of a Commonwealth and who, every four years, invite me around the world to open their games and make small talk with them. On the negative side, I'm married to a man who is balding badly, doesn't much favour people with a darker complexion and doesn't carry too bright a torch for the poor, either. And I'm expected to make small talk as a profession? Well, stuff that for a game of soldiers. Next time someone asks me how I'm bloody doing, I'm going to tell them: 'Better than you. I'm the fucking Queen. Are you going to serve wine at this lunch or are we just going to piss around? And while we're at it, could you give Phil the number for that hair stuff that Shane Warne uses? Oh, and the name of a good plastic surgeon so we can sort out Charlie's ears.' Yes, I'll do that."

But she won't, because she has been making small talk for so long that she now knows no better. If only she'd flown the coop when she was younger. Apart from racism, missionaries and the MG, the worst thing England ever afflicted the planet with was the ability to talk without saying anything at all. And when they make large talk, it tends to get a lot of the Queen's subjects killed in foreign lands. The last three big statements made were in 1914, 1939 and at the beginning of the War on Terrorism (or, as George Bush would call it: *The Crusades II – This Time the Christians Win.*)

On dates, we should use neither small nor large talk. Medium talk, now there's the answer. Small talk tells you nothing about the person you are with and big talk has you telling horrid lies that you will end up believing yourself. Medium talk is what you do with your mates in a bar. A quick hello and it's into the meat of what you've been thinking about the whole day: the state of the nation, sport, politics, global warming, what type of paper aeroplane is the best to throw in the office without having anyone in danger of losing an eye, how much dolphin there is in canned tuna that is not dolphin-friendly, what does dolphin taste like, what does baby seal taste like, what is the best hangover cure after a rum binge, is Dubya taking the piss or is he really that stupid, what beer should one drink with fillet steak, how much more can they tax beer before we have to seriously consider taking money from our retirement funds to keep us afloat in the stuff? That is medium talk.

Big talk is when we gossip and tell lies and half-truths about women. Apart from the notable exception of this book, big talk is what men use when they want to describe what the perfect woman looks like. Medium talk is the language they use when they actually get around to speaking to their perfect woman, because the last thing you want to do with a perfect woman is lie to her. At some time or another she will remind you of the lie, even if you have long since forgotten it.

Small talkers have the longest of introductions. Just saying hello will take up half the date.

"Hi."

"How are you?"

"I'm great. How are you?"

"I'm good. You're good?"

"Yes, very good… so, it's all good then, is it?"

"Uh huh, couldn't be better. I'm feeling great."

"That's great. And how was work?"

"Work was good. You have a good day at work?"

"Yes. Thanks for asking."

"No, I'm glad I asked. Thank you."

In medium chat, an introduction is a single hello from each party and then straight into the meat of conversation. Having something to say on a date can be hard work for the stupid and they will stick with small talk, but the more intelligent of you, who have got this far through what is not that thick a book, are obviously well read and suitably informed about the important and the silly. This is the meat and drink of medium talk.

"Hey."

"Hey back at you."

And that, good people, is an introduction. From here you dive straight into the drinks orders, and then, after the all-important "you're looking good", slip into a brief description of the bar/restaurant. Do not launch into it, this will frighten off perfect women and make them think you are a big-headed nonce, and never say that any place does the "best" of everything. There are no definites in life, not even when it comes to the perfect woman. Once you have made something the "best", you are basically stuffed when it comes to finding somewhere else to go on a second and third date. For example, if a certain place does the "best" pizza and, having taken your date there on an earlier date, you decide to go somewhere else for a pizza, your date will wonder why you are taking her to somewhere with an inferior pizza. She will worry about it from the moment you walk in the door until you go home. Does he think I am not worthy of the best pizza in town, she will fret. Is he going to tell me over a shared supreme with extra garlic that he no longer thinks that we should see each other? If he's taking me to another pizza place, who is he taking to have the best pizza in town? Hey, if this pizza isn't the best, then I'll be buggered if I'm going to let him make me pay for half of it.

I once went to a cocktail bar in a hotel with a group of friends who lured me there under the pretence that the place did the "best" strawberry daiquiris in town. "They use real strawberries," they said in the breathless tone of people who discuss the flavour of alcopops. And indeed they did use fresh strawberries, taking them from a mound that was kept in full view of the rest of the bar to press home the point that they were fresh and they were real. A squish and a blend later and we all had big milkshake glasses of them.

"Aren't they the best you've tasted?" asked the only other single girl in the group, whom I was uncomfortably finding out had been invited to meet me with the hope that we would hit it off.

"It is now. I've never had a daiquiri before. It will be the best I have ever had until I have another one," sucking it so hard and quickly through my straw that my brain froze and I got an ice-cream headache. I finished it and called the barkeep closer.

"My man, do you serve the 'best' beer in town here?" I asked.

"Depends, sir. What's the best beer in town?" he asked.

"The best beer, my man, is not just a cold one. It is the very next one you will serve me from that vast fridge of yours. And after I have finished with that one, the next beer you plop in front of me will be the best one yet again. The best is the best is the best."

"Indeed it is, sir," he said, impressed in a quiet way. "You know, sir. If you and this young lady do not hit it off I have a daughter I'm trying to get rid off. She's not the best, but... "

I held up my hand. "I know, I know, but she may be the best for me right now. At this moment in time, squire," I said, draining a bottle of the best, "find me another best beer and make it the best you've served at this time of night."

"Best I do that, sir."

"Best you do."

The young lady was suitably impressed and ordered herself another of the best daiquiris she had ever tasted. After a few hours of medium talk and some drinks, we bested our inhibitions and had a grand time until the wee hours. It was not the best time, I must admit, but it was fun.

WHERE TO GO

Venues for dates should be places that serve a variety of great things and have something memorable about them. Know where you are going on a date and if there is some history there for your perfect woman, as I have found out to my cost. I told a lady I was most interested in a place I liked going because it had a cosy pub and a fine adjoining restaurant. As I was building up the confidence to ask her if she would like to join me there for a drink and possibly dinner, she cut me off by declaring that she loathed the place, as she had once walked past and seen her ex-husband having a drink. She hasn't spoken to me since because she thinks I am her ex-hubby's drinking partner. It was a hard lesson learned, although some places can toss up unexpected surprises.

On my first date with the Barbie doll – a woman I thought was perfect in a sense – I suggested we go to a place that was neither bar nor restaurant, but a trendy place that was frequented by media types, advertising cokeheads, photographers and other arty types. It wasn't pretentious, served a mean cold beer, had a decent wine list and didn't shut until 4am. They also, I believe, had a very good coffee machine, but I have never gone out to drink coffee because of the senselessness of the very concept of "meeting for coffee". If you need a reason to meet someone, then coffee, a beverage that goes cold and varies in quality from venue to venue, is not a good enough reason.

As we were meeting directly after work, we drove to the café in our own cars. I, nervous as a lamb, had showered at the office, changed my T-shirt and put on long trousers, and the faintest whiff of cologne. I got there early and sat in my car for 30 minutes, watching to see when she would arrive. When she did, I stepped out of my car just after her and pretended to have arrived at the same time. It was pathetic, I know, but she seemed relieved that I was there at the same time as her and didn't have to walk into the venue alone. We walked into the café, a converted house in a street of converted houses, and the waitress asked me if I wanted my usual table. I told her she must be mistaking me for someone else and pushed the Barbie doll past the reception, which would have been the lounge when it was a house, towards a table near the window before that damn waitress reminded me I hadn't paid my tab for that month yet and it was nearing an indecent amount.

We sat down and, after a pushing a stray lock of that gold-spun hair behind her ear, my date told me she had been very pleasantly surprised that I had asked her out.

"What made you send me that email?" she asked, knowing full well that the only reason I had asked her out via email was because she had told one of the girls in the office that she wouldn't be averse to me asking her out. It was a trick question. I hate trick questions.

"Because it seemed like the right thing to do," I smiled.

"Hmmmm, the right thing? What was right about it for you?"

Christ, I thought, she knows how to medium talk. Small talk has been kicked in the nuts. She wasn't all that blonde after all. The Barbie doll was taking the piss now and I felt like Ken: short, plastic and with no dick. I bought myself a second as I gathered my thoughts.

"Honestly?"

"I should hope so."

"Because we meet at all these functions and parties and you're always working. I realised that I don't know anything about you and wanted to talk to you."

Then I almost knocked over my beer, making the Doll and me both shriek. She because she thought I was going to spill beer on her work suit; me, well, because it was beer. The tension eased with that. Nothing breaks tension like clumsiness. We medium-talked ourselves silly. I found out that she had broken up with her boyfriend, who had loved her dearly and had planned the rest of their lives together. She was not ready to head down that path just yet and had plans to run her own public relations company. I thought all of her ideas were great, but then I was dazzled by her face and her voice. They were spectacular, especially her eyes. I wonder how she gets flecks of silver in her eyes and her hair so… she'd stopped talking and was looking around the room.

"Why did you choose this place?"

"I've been here a couple of times before," I said. "It's a chilled place, and… "

"Yes, yes, I know all that," she snapped lightly. "You know I'm connected to this place, don't you?"

"Er… no."

"My grandparents used to live here when this was a house. This was the front bedroom, I think. Hmmm… yes it was. My mother was born in this house."

"In the front bedroom?"

"Yes, I think so. Yes." (She said "yes" a lot.)

"You don't think the actual birthing bed would have been round about here somewhere, do you? What if we're having drinks where your grandma's water broke? And eating pizza where your mum's umbilical cord was cut? That's a bit freaky."

She laughed, which is still the best way to a woman's heart. I had her, and spun out the joke about how the people at the table next to us could be sitting on the chair where the hot water and towels had been put by the midwife. The couple on the other side of the room may have been where her grandpa had stood outside the door to get him out of the way. The next couple of hours flew past. We made plans to meet again. She was nervous, though, and hit me with a request on the way out the door.

"Don't tell my boss. She won't like it at all. Actually, can we keep this just between the two of us for now? People might start talking," she said. It was our first date and yet I felt like I was having an affair with a married woman. "My ex-boyfriend is a bit possessive and if he hears he won't understand. I really enjoyed myself. I do want to see you again."

I promiscd faithfully and offered to walk her to her car. As we stepped outside I heard the magic words, "Hey, McCallum you wanker!" A journalist from another newspaper was sitting at one of the tables outside and called us across. He said hello to the Barbie doll, asked what we were doing together ("Just having a chat," she said) and told us how drunk he was. We left and, when I next bumped into him a few days later, I asked him not to tell anyone about seeing me and the Doll out on the town. "Oh, when was that?" he asked. "At the bar the other night." "Mate, I had to be carried home that night, plus someone had slipped me some acid. I don't remember a thing. So, how long have you and the Doll been going out?"

Now the Doll was regarded as something of a prize in my circle. Public relations and event girls are appraised and graded according to a set of attributes, of which facial make up and body structure are 50 per cent of the score. I know of a PR company that employs only women, and the owner freely admits that looks are very important. The men who run the marketing departments she works with obviously agree because her company does very, very well. The Doll was up there and she knew it, but she did not want others to know we were going out because she felt people may feel she was being unprofessional in seeing me; that I may be a conflict of interest. I'd never been a conflict of interest before and I didn't like it. Conflicts aren't interesting. People get hurt in conflicts and I had an early suspicion that I was going to be the one to get hurt.

The Doll was probably the first girl I went on conventional dates with over a prolonged period of time. It never felt forced, but it was clandestine and never comfortable. She didn't tell anyone at the office, although they eventually found out. She didn't tell her family, because they loved her ex-boyfriend and weren't happy with her for breaking up with him, especially as she had moved back home. I never got to meet her friends, and she missed my birthday party at the bar we'd first kissed at. It was all a little weird.

In many ways, the manner in which I dated her was the way a teenage boy would court a girl. We petted heavily, to use a teenage phrase, in her car. We did so at a drive-in movie, three hours of petting so heavy that we only noticed afterwards that her bum had switched on the hazard lights and they had been flashing for some time.

I don't rightly remember why we broke up, but we did so

without conflict, although I was badly hurt.

Another place I didn't choose as carefully for a first "date" was an ex-girlfriend's flat after a group of us had gone there for post-work drinks. Newspaper journalism has changed and there is not nearly as much drinking as there used to be a decade or so ago. Post-work drinks would start at 11pm, after the paper had gone to bed, and often involve an impressive amount of liquor, which would appear from nowhere ("nowhere" being the editor's office, which we would break into after he had gone home) and then fuel us until about 2am. After one such session we headed to the ex-girlfriend's flat. At about 5am everyone, save for me and the girl I had had a crush on in the office for four months, was asleep.

I asked her if she wanted a drink and went into the kitchen to fetch it. She followed me, put her hand on my neck and we kissed. I had just been jumped in the kitchen of my ex-girlfriend. It doesn't get much stranger but, of the few women I have loved, she was the one who could medium talk the best and we were together for almost two years before she dumped me for the guy she "became aware" of at a party at her ex-boyfriend's flat. Karma, right? Well, karma sucks.

Sports bars are not good places for dates, but they are not as bad as sports venues. I still maintain, to this day, that at the 1995 Rugby World Cup final at Ellis Park in Johannesburg, there were at least 10 000 tickets that went to waste because men were forced to take their wives with them. Do they still talk about that day in June as the best day in their lives? Do they think how lucky they were to be a part of the 62 000 inside the stadium while 40 million South Africans, especially me, had to make do with televisions in bars around the country? Could they, given a rugby ball and a pair of boots, walk onto the field at Ellis Park and find the very spot where Joel Stransky kicked the final drop goal from? No they cannot. There were some very misguided men out there who had the chance to celebrate the day with their friends and they choked badly.

Women who like sports do so because they fancy the look of the players on the field. They do not care for rucks and mauls, unless their fella is at the bottom of it and is getting a line of studs raked down his back. Why would you take a woman on a date where she has a choice of flesh more toned and muscled than yours? It would be the same as her taking you to a strip club. Do not do it, particularly if she knows nothing about cricket and I am the person sitting in front of you, because you know and I know that she is going to ask stupid questions and sooner or later one of us is going to get angry.

"Why do both teams wear white? How do you tell them apart?"

"Why is he rubbing the ball on his balls?"

"What happens, say, if he hits it in the air, but there's that no-ball thingy and someone in the crowd catches it and throws it back to the fielder really quickly before the umpire notices? Is he still out?"

"Do you want some suntan cream on your shoulders?"

"Do you think you should really drink another beer?"

"I'm bored. I wish I'd brought a book."

"Is it nearly finished yet?"

"Sarah just called and she's here, but she hasn't got a seat. Can she squeeze in beside us?"

Sports bars are not as hectic because the sort of women

who go there have some knowledge of sport and know enough to keep quiet enough while you watch it. A friend's wife, who has been trying to hook me up with a variety of her friends for years and years, thought it would be a good idea for me, her and her husband, both of them dear friends of mine, to go to a sports bar to watch the Bulls play Western Province. I thought this a good idea, too, until she called me that morning to tell me that she would be bringing along a friend who I really should meet and who she thought would be perfect for me. This sounded good except for a couple of things. As a professional sports journalist I do not get to support a team all that often. Cheering in the press box is strictly a no-no, although there are a few provincial journalists who feel little to stand up and celebrate when their team scores. But cheering is just not done. You are expected to keep a cap on it, and channel that emotion into your match analysis. Sometimes, when deadlines are tight and you have to file 700 words of copy five minutes after the final whistle, you watch the game out of the corner of your eye and don't actually get to enjoy it. Which is why, when I get the chance to watch a game away from the press box, I tend to get a bit carried away.

Sports bars and in front of my big telly at home are the places where I tend to get carried away, usually when no-one is watching, or when I am with people who know me well enough not to care. But meeting a potential perfect woman while I was trying to watch sport? It could only end in beers and tears. I got to the bar a touch late to find that a place had been left for me between the person I absolutely should meet, and the wife. It was a set-up, an ambush. I would have to talk to one of the two of them no matter what, perhaps even after the whistle had gone to start the game. There was no fobbing her off onto the wife during the game. I stopped in the entrance to the bar and turned to run, but she had seen me and called me across the bar, her voice piercing the mumble of drinkers.

I walked over slowly, my face fixed with the look of a man who is about to crash his car, and sat down between them. My mate looked up from his beer, smiled and shrugged an apology. He ordered me a beer and his wife said, "Kevin has such an interesting job, you know. He's a sports writer."

"Really?" said the friend, who knew only too bloody well what I did for a living. The bloody Saturday newspaper, with my bloody picture by-line was on the bloody table turned towards her. To her credit, she never said "That's interesting" or asked if me if I knew any famous sportsmen. She did ask when I was going to get a real job, which endeared me to her because I have no intention of ever getting a real job. I get paid to watch sport, drink beer and travel the world. I know that what I do has no business being called employment nor do I feel any shame about that. I wear shorts and a T-shirt to work during the summer and on hot winter days. The only time I wear a shirt with a collar is when there is a chance of getting free beer at a black-tie function. My favourite drink is a free beer. My second favourite drink is another free beer.

My date admitted that she did know who I was and hoped I was as funny as my column that morning. I had a quick glance at the paper to see what or who I had slagged off, and found that I had actually been nice to the disabled for a change. Having covered two Paralympic Games and having got stupidly drunk with wheelchair basketball players, I have been given licence to tell jokes about the disabled. My favourite is: what do disabled strippers wear? Crutchless panties. The column that morning had recounted the story of how a friend with polio had been standing outside a shop waiting for his wife to come out. He was leaning on his crutches, holding a can of Coke when a middle-aged lady came past him, stopped and dropped some coins into his half-finished drink. "I think you people are so brave," she had said loudly in case the crutches had made him deaf. My friend looked down at his drink, stared back at the woman, who was patting him on the shoulder and told her politely, "Fuck off, stupid."

It had got a laugh from the date, and I regaled her with more tales of the disabled, including a famous wheelchair athlete who tried to ride his chair down the steps from a lap-dancing bar in King's Cross in Sydney. But the game was getting close and the beers were half full. We would need at least two more each to see us through the first half, and I asked if anyone would like another drink before the game. My friend nodded silently and agreed, his wife pointed out that we already had enough and should wait until halftime. My date went up in my estimation again, by saying: "I'm buying. Would you like another drink, Kev?" Well, beautiful, I didn't come here for a haircut.

We went to the bar, I did the double order and refused to take her money. I have some standards. We sat down, I smiled at her and she thanked me. I was feeling warm things, and I had only had one pot. The teams ran out, the game started and the referee, nervous as hell, bricked his first decision of the match. "Fucking twit," muttered my date. My head turned, a little shock and a little smile. A woman who can use a good curse is worth her weight in gold, and one that likes sport is a platinum chick. Her face was set, her jaw stern and her eyes fixed to the screen. The scrum collapsed as the scrumhalf delayed the feed and the two front rows felt each other out. At the re-set, the Bulls tighthead hit his opposing loosehead at an angle, destroying the Province scrum. "Go you good thing!" I cheered, and felt my cheek getting hot.

"Who do you fucking support, anyway?" she asked gently.

"No-one," I simpered. "I don't have a team. I just know the prop pretty well. He's had a helluva time of it with injury recently and I'm chuffed to see him back."

"You have to support a team, no matter what," she hissed. "You have to pick sides. You can't fuck around with any player from any team you like. I've supported Province ever since I was a kid. I've loved them through thick and thin."

Across the table, I caught my mate's eye and laughed. He giggled back and his wife gave us a bitchy stare. He knew what was coming and she suspected it. I began drinking fast and quickly, supporting the Blue Bulls, not something I would ever do when sober or unprovoked, but the madness had taken me. I became the biggest Bulls fan outside of Loftus. My date became my hate.

At halftime, my mate escaped to the bogs with me. "I know what you're doing and it's damn funny. I should have warned you about her. She's a little psycho when it comes to certain things. She's very competitive, and can be a right bitch. My advice? Get trashed and run after the final whistle. Her last boyfriend did and is still going. The missus thinks she has good qualities, but two drinks and she becomes a nutter. Oh, and thanks for that two-beer trick in the first half. Could you do it again for the second?"

The 40 minutes of the second half are the most liberating I have ever had watching sport. Supporting a team I didn't support just to be a vindictive bastard. Mind you, the Irish have been doing that for years. We fought in the Anglo-Boer war just to get a chance to have a pop at the Poms.

The final whistle went, but the Bulls lost and the adrenaline seeped out of me. To my left was the happiest woman I have ever seen. Like most women who are not used to winning at sports, though, she did not know how to win with grace and carried on about how crap a sports journalist I was and how I knew nothing about rugby. I agreed, nodded my head and said that I had to go as I had to wash my hair tomorrow. "What's wrong? Can't take it, huh? You Bulls fans are all the same. You know, you look a lot shorter in real life." It was a pity, she was so pretty.

HORROR DATES

What can go wrong on a date? Well, everything, actually, from getting too drunk to talking too much, or too little, or choosing the wrong place and time to go on a date. Some of my dearest friends have shared with me their horror dates, begging me to keep their names out of this book. Their tales are all true and much more appalling than anything I have ever been through or, hopefully, will ever go through.

There are so many potential pitfalls for daters and, like eating too much fibre for breakfast, dating can take a lot more out of you than it puts in. Still, we date because we are lonely, horny and because our friends tell us it's the right thing to do.

The "Just Say No" Date

"The first date I went on after my divorce, I was nervous, excited, everything. I imagined kissing him good night after the date – this was a big deal for me after ten years with one man! We met for a drink and I was pleased when he suggested we have supper too – I took it as a sign that things were going well. But then he kept going to the loo, very often, and when he got back to the table in between trips he'd speak very fast, mostly about Marxism. Being a bit uncertain of myself I thought I was being a bit slow in keeping up with the conversation, and that he was very clever.

"Finally he came back from one of the trips to the loo and told me the cleaning woman in there was very cross with him, and when I asked why he said because he had been vomiting a lot. I felt very sorry for him and asked where he thought he could have picked up the bug, and he said he wasn't sure. After a bit, he suggested we make a quick stop at the chemist so he could get something for it before we resumed our date. The chemist was closed, as it was late, so we drove to another one, which was also closed.

"Then his vomiting got really bad and he asked me to take over driving. He had a really good idea of where all the chemists in the city were situated, which in retrospect should have aroused my suspicions. I had to drive really slowly and stop every few hundred metres so he could vomit. After a while he asked me to take him to an emergency ward at a hospital, all the time telling me what a fantastic woman I was because I was so nurturing and kind.

"We got to the hospital at midnight, and he told the nurse exactly what sort of drip he needed (still no suspicions on my part) and then I sat in the waiting room for a while.

When he came out, looking fine, he suggested going on somewhere for coffee. I said okay, I have no idea why. So we had coffee and ice cream and he took me home and, as he leaned across to kiss me good night, I dodged and darted out of the car to avoid his vomit breath.

Later someone told me that he'd told her that he thought I was fantastic, that he thought we may get married one day, and that he'd taken a lot of heroin on our date."

There are good lessons here, people. Don't do class-A drugs on a first date. And if your date happens to jolly off to the lavatory more times in one night than you do in a week, wait until they go for the tenth time then skip out of the bar and run for your life.

The "Talk to Me about Your Brother" Date
"I went out with two brothers (not at the same time). Brother One was playing in a band at a bar, and I was there with friends. After they'd played, he came over and chatted and I laughed at his jokes. He vaguely knew one of my friends and phoned her the next day for my number. We went out for a drink where he talked a lot about himself.

"He told me he'd achieved absolutely nothing that day at work, which was a problem because, as a lawyer, you bill by the hour. I said not to worry, I'd had those days, and sometimes you just needed to write it off and start over again the following morning. He said that was all very well but he'd not been able to bring himself to work for eight months. He didn't ask me a single thing about myself so, when he suggested we meet up again, I was surprised. I've been on many dates since, though, and now know that this is not an unusual thing.

"Brother Two, it so happens, asked me out the same week. It was a weird coincidence, as I didn't know they were brothers. I gatecrashed a party by mistake, and he was the deejay. When I realised I was at the wrong party (it was hideous, I saw my therapist), I went to the real party. Then, later on, I went back to the wrong party because it was more fun and I was drunk. Brother Two also vaguely knew my friend, and asked for my number the next day. She told him I had already been out with his brother but that didn't matter to him. For our date, he suggested we go swimming at a public pool and I refused, knowing it was mistake right from the start. I eventually turned up with a 'rock chick' T-shirt and a very bad attitude."

What can we glean from this particular episode? Well, for one, dating siblings is not a great idea. Also dating losers, who aren't afraid to tell you they're losers, is not a great idea. Conversely, you should avoid dating your sibling's ex and losers. Moreover, if you know a date is a fundamentally bad idea, just don't do it.

The "What's That Smell" Date

"I once went out with a man who, during the course of the dinner, told me he worked for a company that manufactured fragrances for loo fresheners and things. Later, he mentioned that the fragrances were very concentrated and he'd unfortunately spilt some in his car. 'Ah, that explains the smell!' I exclaimed, a little relieved. He looked at me funny and said what he had meant was that he split the scent several months prior… so the smell was his aftershave. The date sort of petered out after that… "

No major lesson here, really. Except, maybe, don't wear crap cologne.

CHRISTIANS AND DATING

This isn't the same as horror dating, but it isn't a sinful mile away. If you are a fundamentalist Christian – and there are far too many out there for my liking, or indeed the good of the world – dating creates all sorts of spiritual and ethical problems. As it is, dating has enough pitfalls and rules that many of us will never understand or bother to learn because, just as soon as you do, they change again in the blink of a large beer being poured. But for fundamentalist Christians, it must be a nightmare.

(I am picking on my people here so as to avoid the burning of this book by other fundamentalist groups should I, say, wish to include a cartoon to illustrate what a deity would do on a date. I make jokes about Christianity and Jesus, because I am sure that up on high, or wherever Jesus hangs around these days, he doesn't much approve of what the Christians have been getting up to. The rubbish that is done in the name of Jesus and that other prophet whose name begins with an "A" is frightening.)

Because most Christians have been brought up with Western values, the date is a field packed full of sexual land mines for them. On a website I stumbled across whilst searching for the perfect woman, a worried young Christian man asked, "Are we supposed to be actively looking for a spouse, or waiting for God to bring a spouse to us?" He was given a roundabout answer that included the line, "The answer is to both is yes… in a way. Let's look at the very first marriage. God made Adam, then Eve, brought them together and married them. Adam didn't need to go out searching for the perfect woman. God knew who would be best for him, so He brought her to him… In the New Testament, we are given guidelines for what to look for in a mate, but are not told specifically how to go about finding one."

So, lucky Adam, although one supposes that he had to have God bring him his bird. It's not like there was an Irish theme bar in the Garden of Eden for him to go carousing to pick up someone on a Saturday night. Besides, as it was just the two of them, who would serve them shooters? The serpent? Would the bar have a clothing policy and a minimum age? These are all important questions, and ones that keep me awake some nights when closing hour has come upon me unexpectedly. As Christians do not condone drinking (although they conveniently forgot that Jesus turned barrels of water into wine), this makes dating all the more difficult, as the website went on to tell this unbeliever, especially as there are no stories about dating in the good Book.

"There are many downfalls to dating in search of a partner in our society now. Dating is not found in the Bible and is not a biblical concept at all. The young years are not supposed to be the time to 'sow your oats' before you get ready to settle down; they're supposed to be a time to grow spiritually (Luke 1:17). All too often the subject around youth groups becomes 'who likes who' and 'who's dating who' instead of figuring out how to reach spiritual maturity. Another thing to think about is the emotional toll dating can take on a person. The past heartbreaks and perhaps regretted intimate moments can infect the future relationship you have with your spouse."

Hmmm, there's some wisdom in that last statement, even if it does smack of being rather chicken-shit reasoning. Don't date in case you get hurt? That's like saying, don't play rugby in case you get tackled, don't score a goal in football in case you never do it again and feel worthless for the rest of your sad, troubled life? Why, for instance, do Italy continue to enter the Six Nations when they know they are going to get thumped every year? Because dating, like rugby, football and other contact sports is a bizarre kind of fun.

A TIP FROM HOLLYWOOD

As an individual who managed to convince two girls to kiss in *Starsky and Hutch* and used weddings to meet women, actor Owen Wilson is a man whose advice should be treated with respect. He has, he says, "well-rehearsed dating techniques" to "speed up his quest for his perfect woman". "My best dating tip: pretend to be a good listener. Express an interest in movies like *Mystic Pizza*, *Steel Magnolias* and *Ghost*. Be romantic like with candlelit dinners by the fireplace – stuff that girls like. Who knows? One day maybe I'll be lucky enough to meet a great girl and get married and start a family."

Of course, Owen. Except that the women you hang out with have probably starred in the movies that you want us to watch with them. What movies do Hollywood stars rent when they want to cuddle in front of a television? Each other's movies? Maybe taking advice from a movie star is not such a good idea.

FUNDAMENTAL DATING

Right-wingers neither make good dates nor do they conform to what makes a good date. (Nor, as I have pointed out above, do fundamentalist Christians.) I'm sure they would make perfect women for men who cannot think for themselves, or who have been storing up cans of beans for the day when they take over the government.

While having drinks with a girl who looked sane on the outside, she told me that it was so nice that I had chosen a bar with no "blacks" in it. I had a quick squiz and she was right, but it was a drinking spot that was usually rather cosmopolitan.

"Don't you think that the blacks are taking all the best jobs from the whites?" she continued.

"Only from those whites who weren't very good at their jobs in the first place," I answered, ordering the bill from our black waitress and over-tipping her horribly.

"Yes, but our country was so much better before they took over," she whined as I walked her to my car, where the black security guard was waiting for his tip, and the black car washer was polishing my windscreen.

The only person she hated worse than people of colour were gays and left-wingers. Possibly, I suggested, that was because they dressed better than her (gays not left-wingers) and listened to better music. Plus, they all liked black people. "Yes," she said, putting Snoop Dogg on the car's CD, "but they don't have the values that you and I have." The way her hand moved up my thigh and on to my groin suggested she wanted to add to the white race, but racists tend to turn me off.

I have dated girls who I have found out are strict Christians only after they have had a couple of sharp drinks. Christian girls who get drunk can be more friendly than your standard heathen. The latter is already damned to hellfire and, in accepting this, is constantly on the outlook for more and better ways to sin. Sex with heathens is good, but you have to be constantly inventive with them. With Christians, who don't get out all that often, it's a lot easier to titillate them. If you are not a bad boy, then you have to act like one.

A few years ago, I organised a party at my house to watch the league cup final and, as well as several colleagues from work and my brothers, asked a girl involved in event management business I had met at a cricket match to come along. She was tall, blonde and had a good giggle on her. I was short, had black hair and had a wiggle on me. I thought we would be a good match.

The night before I went to a friend's house, which was a mistake. I knew it was a mistake as soon as I went through to the back garden and saw the host slip into his koi fish pond. I had played football, hockey and cricket with these lads for over ten years and had had done many silly things with them. We were drinkers, hard drinkers and the parties we had together were just downright daft. At one end-of-season football party, a player's girlfriend arrived to find four naked guys standing around the braai. The dog had been taught how to fetch six-packs from the pool (even though he would pierce the cans with his teeth and have them fizz down his throat. That poor dog was hammered at the end of the evening). And that the owner of the house and myself were sumo wrestling with tea towels tied around our nether regions. I remember that party well. Entry was a case of beer and two bottles of shooters each. On the night in question, the Buffalo Rule was, as always, in effect, where you had to drink with your left hand only. Anyone caught drinking with the right hand had to down what they had in their bottle. There were penalties for not conforming to other rules. Saying "beer" was banned – you had to use the phrase "reeb" instead. It was that silly.

As you do, I woke up in the lounge of my friend's place mid-morning, wandered outside to where the other drunks were sitting around the embers of what had been the biggest fire in history the night before. I got myself a breakfast beer and joined them. Four hours later I got a call from my brother telling me that a girl had arrived at my house and said she knew me. When was I coming home? I got home an hour later in showroom condition to find that my brother's wife had taken over the catering. I drank more and flirted with the tall blonde, who was getting tipsy on wine and cider. The game finished, my team won and she shrieked in all the wrong places, but I was too blurry to notice. Then, like Cinderella, she looked at her watch and said she had to run. I saw her to her car and she told me what a wonderful time she had had. I agreed, reminding myself to ask my friends to remind me of what a good time I had had when I was sober.

Ten minutes after walking inside, the phone rang and my brother answered it. "It's for you," he shouted.

"Hello? Is this Kevin?" said an old lady.

"Yes."

"Has my daughter left there yet? She has to go to church tonight. She wasn't drinking, was she?"

"No," I lied. I never saw that girl again after that. Being tipsy in church is not a good thing.

One Good Friday, when I was down at the pub having a quiet lunchtime beer for Jesus, I had a good idea for a joke and SMSed it to friends. "Don't you think it was very nice of Jesus to die on public holiday?" I sent it to an Australian girl I had met on my travels abroad, thinking she would appreciate it. Within a minute, the Brisbane Babe had replied, indignant. "I can't believe u said that! What do we have if we don't believe in anything?" We have, I replied, ourselves. Those of you who need something else to believe in have already lost that belief.

Girls who love politicians should also not be trusted or wooed. A female friend of mine told me that one of her friends had dated a man who told her he woke up every day and thanked God for George W Bush because he had saved the world.

On an internet dating blog I visited, a man recounted the story of how he had met a statuesque stunner who had certain requirements of her perfect match. "As God is my witness," wrote the blogger, "there is an ad on Match.com from MissNorway98 [her screen name] who, based on her picture, is absolutely stunning. But the text from her ad stunned me more: 'You will lose points if you suggest we watch Michael Moore's *Fahrenheit 9/11*. I can't think of anything that would turn me off more. Also, if your profile describes you as 'Liberal' or 'Very Liberal,' we are clearly not a Match. I am more concerned about your mind than your body. Big muscles will not impress me, but sincerity and patriotism will. If you oppose the foreign policy of the United States then you are not for me. A guy who believes the United States was wrong to intervene in Afghanistan and Iraq is not for me. America liberated my country from the Nazis, and we have not forgot."

Right then…

CONCLUSION

Let there be no doubt that dating is hard. Sometimes, during a date you will feel like the Americans did when they got into Vietnam and how they currently feel about the war in Iraq. You shouldn't be there. There must be a better way of finding the perfect woman than the stress of a setting up a meeting at which you are expected to perform at a certain standard in order to take the relationship to another level. Dating is like the national military service that some countries force their young adults to go through. It's the best time of your life that you wish did not have to happen.

5

I KNOW JUST THE PERSON

The perfect woman is beautiful, Russian, friendly and wants me so badly it will only cost me a couple of thousand dollars to fly her over to my place. I know this because she tells me so: *Congratulations my new friend!!!! I saw your structure. And I loved your description on your structure. I'm nice russian girl. I think you like me!!! Because I'm very funny girl. I dream to get acquainted for serious attitudes with kind, decent, cultural and clever the man. The output for husband is possible. I live in Russia in not big city Volzhsk. In this city there are* *many beautiful places where it is possible to have rest. I in a life the cheerful person with sense of humour, the good blonde. My growth of 172 sm, weight of 59 kg. For these 32 years I could not find second half with whom I could divide other life. What to create happy and safe family. I work in a kindergarten as the instructor. And almost I spend I all time with children. With this letter I shall send you a photo. We could closer acquaint and study each other better. But on it it is necessary during a lot of time. On it I shall be closed, and I shall wait from you for the answer. With the following letter I shall send you still photos. I wish all of you the most good. Sincerely yours to you the new friend from Russia Guzel!!!*

This is taken verbatim from a dating website and after looking at the picture of what must be the most beautiful girl in the world, I thought that "closer acquaint and study each other better" was as good an offer as I have had in a while. As a kind, decent, cultural and clever man, I think I deserve a young Russian girl and want to do "serious attitudes" with her. So do many other desperate men for whom the search for a perfect woman has just got too much. Not long after I stumbled across this profile, I read a report that internet dating websites were sending out frantic warnings to clients that there was a syndicate tapping up lonely men for money by luring them with the promise of, let's be honest, a Siberian shag.

The "girls" tell blokes who double click on their profiles that they love the look of their balding heads and beer bellies, and would love to come to visit them in their country, where they could have some serious attitudes and get to know each other better. If only, the little Ivana pouts, she had the money to fly to see them. As it is, they need $200 to pay the landlord because he is threatening to kick her on to the street but, woe is them, they don't know where to get it. They so wish they were near such a kind, decent and cultural man, who will, no doubt, have a kind, decent and cultural bank account from which he could surely spare a few thousand dollars. More men fall for this than you would think. But then there are still Australians falling for Nigerian money scams. There are stupid people the world over.

There are, however, a number of websites offering to put lonely men in touch with Russian women, and not get ripped off. A website, russian-women-info.com, tells you how to "find, meet and marry a Russian woman". It asks the pertinent question, "Are you crazy enough to marry a Russian woman?" Because "dating a Russian woman is not the same like dating a person". The English is shocking, but they warn that there are many pitfalls to Russian women, including the language barrier. You should write an introductory letter to her, but write it in Russian because it will show that you care, is easier for her to read, she won't have to pay for translating it and you will be able to express yourself better because the western sense of humour does not come across well in Russian.

What? You don't speak or write Russian? You're in luck, my friend, because they just happen to offer a translation service that charges per word. But, hey, what is money when you are looking for love. They also recommend that you take a romantic Russian holiday to meet your woman and, yes, they do arrange tours, why do you ask?

Elana Petrova, a tall, skinny woman, met and married a western man back in 1998, and then wrote a book on the topic called *How to Meet and Marry a Woman Like Me.* It has become a best-seller, giving all sorts of advice:

Let you understand what Russian women REALLY want, why do they want it, and how you can give it to them;

Tell you what Russian women fears are and how to deal with them;

Guide you through the hidden traps of Russian courting etiquette;

Tell you what is the biggest turn-off for Russian women in their relationship with western men;

Explain to you about giving gifts and shopping with Russian women;

Tell you which popular western phrase can destroy your perfect relationship in an instant;

Show you the right way to start a sexual relationship with a Russian woman and how to avoid embarrassment if things don't work the way they should;

Explain to you about marriage proposals to Russian women;

Teach you how to survive visa application period and use it to strengthen your relationship;

Show you the ways to ensure the woman is getting married to YOU and not to your country;

Discuss the problems of adaptation and homesickness and what you can do to cure them.

Clever Elana has letters of recommendation from men who have found success in their search for the perfect Russian woman. One of those is from an author by the name of Michael Mullen, who found his love through the methods outlined by Elana. Mullen may not be the best of men to take advice from, however. He wrote the book *War*

I Know Just the Person

of the Angels, a work of non-fiction or, as he describes it, "a true story of extraordinary supernatural experiences and prophecies". In it he "recounts numerous occasions spanning the past quarter century, when the author was pulled from his body and transported to a vast Dark World, where angels from opposing forces battled. The leader of the heavenly angels, whose face appears in the burial shroud of Turin, told Michael [that's him, the author] to write what he saw. The leader of the evil angels, a beast, threatened to kill the author and his family if he ever published War of the Angels." He did and, to the best of my knowledge, he is still alive. He may even still be married to a Russian girl.

Should one go abroad when looking for the perfect woman? Indeed yes. There is something about a foreign accent that flicks a trigger in females. Young men abroad have been known to use their accents to ensure that they are young men aboard a broad as often as they possibly can. It is well-known that one international sportsman has a calling card that identifies himself as the minister of foreign affairs and he takes it upon himself to spread the goodwill of his country to as many of the women of each of the countries he visits. His success is legendary, and many of his countrymen have found themselves the recipients of affections from the women he has left in his wake. I have been told by an Australian girl that my South African accent is a turn-on for her. She has admitted that when she hears a male South African accent, and there are plenty of them around the world these days, she will linger around making small talk (I have tried to teach her about medium talk, but she is Australian and there is only so much a man can do) to feel the damaged vowels sending tingling feelings through hidden and sensitive bits of her body. Her car broke down and her repairman was a South African who had relocated to Australia. She told me that she spent an hour talking to him about pistons, intake valves and fuel injection. She once heard a man from Cape Town speaking on a late-night talk radio show and SMSed me to tell me. I take full responsibility for this peculiarity, and have offered to send her a recording of my voice for those moments when she is alone and in need of a vocal seeing-to. She's still trying to make up her mind about it. Should she go for it, I may go into the voice sex business, but I have my doubts that it would provide me with a sustainable income.

Of all the foreign girls I have come across (hang on… you know what I mean), I have found that Australians are the friendliest and amongst the best looking. French girls, particularly the barmaid who once served me at the L'Ascot bar in Monte Carlo, are by far the most beautiful and poised, but also the most difficult to talk to for obvious reasons. Like men who live in South Africa, though, I stand by the women of my fair country being the best-looking in the world. A good friend's wife, a former beauty queen and model, told me this and as she's in the business I have no reason to doubt her judgment. Plus, I have to live in South Africa long after this chapter has been written and, as I will be continuing my search mainly in that country, it would be best if I did not alienate the land's female population.

That said, I do think that a man should go foreign, if only to make himself aware of what he may or may not be missing out on. You may also be doing your country's tourism industry a fine service. In *The Spectator*, the very fine columnist Rod Liddle suggested that the increased, er, friendliness of British girls has had as much to do with the increase in Britain as a tourist destination as has Big Ben or the Queen. While British girls may not be the girls that you will want to sleep with, wrote Liddle, they are no doubt the girls you have already slept with and will sleep with again in the near and distant future. Why? Because you know you can. It is the road well travelled, the path with well-worn ruts, the... ah, you understand. British girls have become "easier" to bed in the latter part of the last century because they have been taking more responsibility for sex instead of just waiting for it to happen to them. Lying back and thinking of your country is all well and good, but thinking of dear England is not easy when they have not won the World Cup since 1966. They could of course get on their backs and think of Martin Johnson's 2003 Rugby World Cup team or the 2005 Ashes winners, but Jonno's fierce eyebrows and Kevin Pietersen's hairstyle may not do it for the Pom chicks.

Liddle is not convinced that it is the evil of binge drinking that has led to British girls being hot to trot, because most of them are up to get well-licked before they get well-liquored. A recent trip to London confirmed that English girls are indeed dressing a lot more skankily these days. There are midriffs bared even during the dead of winter, and I use the phrase midriffs with caution. There are tummies bulging out from under T-shirts that are too tight and bums crammed into jeans stretched until their seams scream for mercy. As a man who buys clothes that fit and, hopefully, flatter the excess that excess has put on my bum and tum, I have never understood the need for women to wear clothes that do nothing for them. Here's a hint, girls. If you are fat, do not

wear Lycra, crop tops or hip-hugging jeans. Your hips have
no need to be hugged, they require shaping under clothes
cut not just of the right cloth, but of enough of it. Until
I drop at least another ten kilograms, you will not see me
wear a muscle T-shirt, nor those 32-inch waist Levi's 501s
that are waiting for me in my cupboard. Yes, I too have fat
clothes and have had cause to wear them a little more often
than I should.

There is a woman I admire greatly for a variety of factors,
not least of which because I probably have a crush on her,
but also because she has a great awareness of her body. While
she is not happy with bits of herself, she knows how to show
off the bits that work really well and, being a gentleman, I
will allow her to catch me surreptitiously appreciating those
bits. The perfect woman will not be totally perfect, but this
is part of the attraction of them. She will have parts of her
that she is desperately unhappy with and will wish to change.
For instance, I had a girlfriend who had just come back
from England and was still recovering from the Heathrow
injection. She was a little round in places, but I did not
see that. I saw her eyes, the sultriest eyes, which changed
shape with her smile. I saw her hair, which had a Chrissie
Hynde-like fringe to it, sitting just above the top of her
upper eyelids. I didn't see past her face, and it was not until
we got naked, on the night of her birthday two days after
we first kissed, that I found she also had a quite lovely set of
boobs. I really liked those boobs, they went so well with her
face and, as we spent most of the first three months of our
relationship naked, I saw the two of them a lot together in
various locations and from various angles. As we went out

and she settled back into South African life, she began to lose weight and, one night as we were lying in bed together, she asked and informed me about the state of her breasts: "My tits are getting smaller now that I'm losing weight?" I didn't know what to say because I hadn't noticed actually. I did not feel a need to comment on her body. Hey, if she wasn't going to comment on the size of my junior, who was I to talk about her tits? Fair was fair, I reckoned.

But I loved her hair. Then she cut it short and got it spiky, and I loved that, too. And I loved her new, small boobs, and her pert bum and tight tum. Then again, I just loved her full-stop, but enough about love. It is a topic we shall explore soon enough.

The point is she knew how to dress to suit her body and her face. All of the women I have liked have known how to dress. It has amazed me, as I'm sure it has them, that when I have come to sleep with some of them they seem to have more and less flesh in various parts when they get their kit off. This is always a delightful surprise, although I am sure that most of them have stopped halfway through the seduction process and thought "How the fuck did he get all of that beer gut underneath that T-shirt?" By careful planning and the use of dark colours, my friends, that's how. If you have got it, don't flaunt it. Disguise it and then dim the lights later. Besides, most of you will be drunk by that stage anyway – an extra or lesser handful here or there will not make much of a difference. Getting naked is always fun, particularly when you don't know what to expect.

Where is just how a lot of British girls are going wrong. Getting your tits out for the lads is all well and good, but only if your tits aren't already out for the lads and they have no wish to see them again. I personally find British girls attractive, but then I was born in Belfast, Northern Ireland and, as with the South African excuse, I may find myself venturing down that path one day as my search goes on. Why are British girls "easy"? Liddle says that they put out because "they are expected to and because there is no reason not to. They are doing what society – and Italian male tourists – expect of them, without fear or fervour. If you think they are wrong-headed in their behaviour, then think quickly and invent a reason for them to change their behaviour. Meanwhile, the rest of Europe can lie back and simply enjoy."

Amen, brother. This is the same reasoning that Australian women and girls, for there is a distinction, use in their approach to sex. They are not easy, to use a horrid phrase, but they do enjoy a shag. I remember reading a dating columnist who, whilst during the act of intercourse with an Australian tourist, had been banging away with what he thought was a skilful bit of hipsway, when he paused momentarily to change tempo. In the millisecond that he stopped, she tapped him on the shoulder and said, "You slimed yet, mate?" He never did. There's a quite rough and ready attitude to sex in Australia, which is strange, but exciting for a wough and weady man such as myself. Australian men have an Are-you-awake-Sheila? attitude to sex and the clitoris is a dish you get down in Sydney's Chinatown after a skinful. During a drunken discussion with an Australian girl about sex, we had concluded that she liked giving blow jobs, liked sitting on top, doggie style, but had never had a man give her oral sex. There are some things an Australian man will not eat. Drunker yet, the subject of anal sex came up and she stopped me dead: "That's one thing I'm saving for my husband. I will not have anal sex until I am married." And do you know, she still hasn't.

I have never slept with an American girl, possibly because of the fear of being sued for not delivering on promises. During a month-long holiday in the United States, my mate Matthew and I went on an extended beer-run down the west coast of the United States, starting in a hick town in northern California called Reading and travelling in a loop that took us through San Francisco, Santa Cruz, San Luis Obispo, Los Angeles, Las Vegas and then back to Reading and San Francisco. We concentrated on drinking more than we did chatting up girls, besides, I had fallen heads over heels for a girl back in South Africa and, even though I hadn't told her about my crush yet, wasn't much interested in American girls. Not that there weren't offers. In San Luis Obispo, we got pissed-oh in a student bar. Matt wore a Springbok rugby jersey, which caught the attention of a really big fella behind the bar. He heard my accent and got talking.

"You from South Africa?"

"Two double Jack and… – yes, I am. Why?"

"I run the local rugby club. We watch you guys on satellite. You guys can play? You play any rugby at all? We need players, man."

"Why, yes. Have you heard of a team called Western Province?"

"Hell yes. You play for them?"

"Almost. We were transferred, 'traded' to Northern Transvaal, though."

Before I knew it, I had promised to stay in town for a week and Matthew and I were going to try out for the local team at the weekend. It got us free drinks the whole night, which, in turn, attracted two of the local students, who told us that they would really like to see our motel room. The offer they gave was explicit, but as I walked outside I managed to not see a massive oak tree and walked straight into it. When I got up the girls were gone.

Our trip went on, through LA and a stay with Matthew's neurosurgeon uncle, Emmy award-winning playwright aunt and family, where we became regulars at a bar called Dublin's on Sunset Boulevard, hustling the occasional B movie actor for money at pool, and on to Las Vegas. On our first night there, we drank our way up the strip, pretending to gamble to get free drinks until, at about 4am, we found ourselves in a lizard lounge populated by 40-somethings who were giving us the eye. Matthew was giving it back, but I had had enough and left him to it, and began the walk back down the strip. I would venture to say that I was impressively drunk and that the only thing keeping me upright was the heat of the place, even at 4am. After an age when I was tiring badly, a blue Pontiac convertible with a big girl at the wheel, pulled up on the road along side me.

"Hey, man, you need a lift?" asked what looked, despite the booze in my eyes, like a really big girl.

"Do I ever," I said, and got into the car. "I'm staying near Caesar's Palace." Off we drove, slowly.

"Where you from?" she asked.

"South Africa," I said.

"South Africa? They have black people like me there?"

"Why, yes, they do."

"So, you looking for a girlfriend?" she asked and I realised just why she had picked up a drunk white boy on a long, empty street.

"Yeeesssss, but, um, not tonight," I stammered.

"You're not a cop are you?" she asked again, and reached over and squeezed my balls through my jeans. "No, you're not," she said. I sat there stunned, freshly squeezed.

"How can you tell?"

"I just can. Are you sure you haven't got $37 for a blow job?"

"No, sorry. I spent all my money on drink." She dropped me off. American girls, I have been told, are easy. Some are easier than others.

One American girl who hasn't found dating as easy as my big friend from Vegas, was Laurie Long, a San Franciscan artist. She had an idea to mix her search for the perfect man with art. She was getting on a bit, having hit the horror of the late 30s with no male prospects in sight, working two jobs so that she could keep calling herself an artist and hadn't had the pleasure of male company for two years. I've seen a picture of her and on looks alone she deserved a date.

"I didn't have time to go looking for love, I was too busy working," she told *The Times*. "The only way was to turn finding someone into a piece of art. This was not a stunt. I wanted a love life. I really did want a relationship."

She began dating with a passion, wearing a camera and a microphone about her person to capture each date. It became an artwork of sorts, called Dating Surveillance Project, where we see Long's dates with men and, in a reality TV-type commentary, going into the toilet to tell how the date was going. She said that the work "combined feminism and humour" because she was "sick of heavy, political work". This from a woman who put her panties into vending machines in galleries as art. She does not say whether she sold many of them.

That's nothing new to us lovers of the bizarre. In Japan used schoolgirl panties are on sale in vending machines all over Tokyo, although it is suspected that there are factories of hairy and sweaty Russian woman stepping into and out of panties, churning out sweaty knickers for the jollies of Japanese businessmen. They sell everything from vending machines in Japan. I was in Kyoto for the 2002 World Cup and went out for a walk to see the ancient temples of the place. Outside one of the most spectacular I saw a bank of vending machines. As well as a drink called Sweat, I could also buy a bottle of Suntory Whisky for 1,500 yen. There were no vending machines that sell perfect women, though, unless your perfect woman is plastic with a valve.

But back to Laurie Long and her camera. Why the subterfuge? "Dating really is like spying. You have to ask indirect questions to find out what you need. For instance, 'Why did you move to San Francisco?' is intended to ascertain whether the man is straight. Every woman I know in this city has dated a man who has had sexual-identity issues. Then find out if he has sisters – it's a big plus: he probably understands women."

Long eventually fell in love – with her housemate. She got to know him and felt comfortable with him before they fell for each other. "It seems a miracle to me that we fall in love despite all the built-in pitfalls. I don't know how we do it. Dating is so artificial, to actually strip away the veneer and get to the real person beneath is so hard. Often people don't have the time to wait around to find out."

LOVE, PERFECTION AND EVERYTHING ELSE

I do not fall in love easily. If I did then it would not be love. There are many different types of love, I have been told, which I am not entirely sure I believe either. If love had so many varieties then, when you lost someone you loved, it wouldn't hurt so much. What some mistake for love is familiarity, which breeds as much content as it does contempt. I have friends who have got married because they became familiar with their girlfriends rather than falling in love with them. Besides, familiars are those mortals that vampires take as their slaves, aren't they? Sluggish Goths who want to be immortal bloodsuckers, which is pretty much like marriage, actually.

Perhaps that is why I am single – because I know what love is and how much it can hurt – and that is why I search so diligently for a perfect woman. Perhaps that is why I hate dating so much, why I detest the frivolity of the way we are forced to seek out mates instead of finding that one great moment of serendipity. Perhaps I expect too much. Yeah, perhaps…

I have told just three women that I have loved them. The others I liked a lot. I remember every single woman who has told me that they loved me, because there have not been a lot of them. I remember well the moment each one of them told me they loved me because I know just how vulnerable it made them feel. One, perhaps the sweetest of all, told me by sending me a document that caused my Mac to crash with a glorious thud. When I opened it, I found that it said: "I think… I'm really falling for you." Another told me by holding my hand in a bar in a quiet corner, and looking me squarely in the eye. I never told her I loved her back and that was a mistake. A girl told me as we were having sex, blurting out "I love you" like a horny bloke would. When I made a move to reply, she stopped me and told me not to say anything I didn't mean. So I didn't because I didn't. She still holds out hope that I will, but I wouldn't do that to her and I hope she understands if she reads this. Another, with whom I had a staggered relationship that involved drink and sex, took me out for a drink and then dumped it on me after she had bought the third round, always a dangerous time for a man, that, the third round. I was honest with her, not brutally honest, but honest enough to save face for her and leave me looking like a fool. I get paid to look like a fool so it wasn't that great a sacrifice after all.

My friends worry horribly about me being single. My dearest female friend, who once confessed to me that she had had a massive crush on me, told me that she was dedicating 2006 to being the Find-Kevin-a-girlfriend year. Many expected she and I would hook up eventually, as she is a perfect girl, but we have the perfect friendship and it would have sent that to buggery on a rocket. Besides, she now has the perfect husband and the perfect son, and she is the perfect friend.

In the process of breaking up with me, a girlfriend told me that I should go out with her sister as she wanted to keep me around. I think, though, that was just her feeling sad for the way she fell out of love with me, perhaps knowing that it would leave me a rather tangled mess for two years. She was one of the few I told I loved.

Who or what is the perfect woman? As this is my book, my definition is the be-all and the end-all within its covers. You may have your own but, if you do not, feel free to use mine.

The perfect woman is a slip of a woman, who probably has a few extra bits and pieces she would rather you didn't talk about. She's a curvaceous girl who would like a bit more in some places she wouldn't mind you mentioning because she thinks it quite funny. She fucks like a tiger, shags like a Sheila and makes love all at the same time. She walks with a sway of her hips that makes her float across the room, looks slightly awkward on high heels but glorious in a little black, backless dress. Her hair changes all the frigging time, and she asks just once whether you like it or not. If you don't then too bloody bad, mate. When she asks if her bum looks big in a pair of pants and you answer in the affirmative, she thanks you for being honest. She makes you tingle when she walks into a room. She makes you horny when she walks into a bedroom. She makes you rich when she walks into a boardroom (not necessary, but it would never hurt, just an optional extra). She does not ask you how your day was because, if either of you wanted to talk about it, then you would have brought it up already. She considers "fuck" one of the best words ever invented, a valid adjective, verb, adverb and noun. She loves Eddie Izzard. And U2. And Blur. And REM. And Fat Boy Slim. And has a better CD collection than you. She has interesting and slightly kooky friends. She has heard of sobriety and thinks that it is a rather cute concept. She understands that beer needs no further discussion. Beer is beer. She will try to persuade you, with the promise of oral sex, to stay home instead of going to play football, and will understand when you accept the oral sex and then rush off to play football before coming home to return the favour. She sets no timetable for your relationship. She does not need your approval.

There is a perfect woman out there for me. I know there is. Will I find her? Probably. Maybe. One day. It will not happen because I want it to. I will, in all likelihood, find her by mistake. Perhaps it will happen by design. Perhaps it will not happen at all. I hope, though, that it does.

Also by Two Dogs...

293 Things Every SA Man Should Know
By Dennis Cavernelis

This is exactly what it says: a compilation of 293 snippets of knowledge for the South African man – from worldly wisdom and indispensable advice to good-humoured observation and trivial facts. But it's not as straightforward as all that… There's zombie-killing advice, jump-starting advice and cigar-lighting advice. There are facts to remember, facts to forget and facts to drop at fancy dinner parties. An ideal gift and even a conversation piece, this is the thinking man's light read.

ISBN 1-920137-01-7

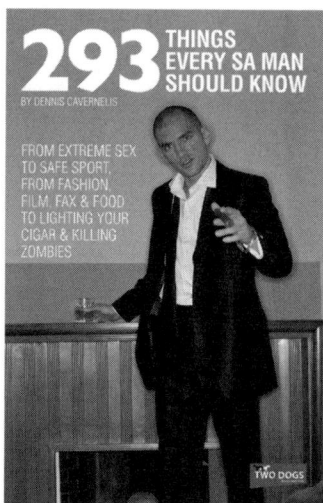

I Can Do That – Fitness for the Lazy Guy
By Blair Ludbrook

This is the book that every stressed out, unhealthy South African guy needs to prod him off the couch and into a healthier lifestyle. Taking a complete approach, it gives readers the knowledge and motivation to take the jump from lazy layabout to half-marathon runner or regular surf-skier – while still enjoying a beer or two. There's no preaching here: just an achievable, practical recipe for success.

ISBN 1-920137-02-5

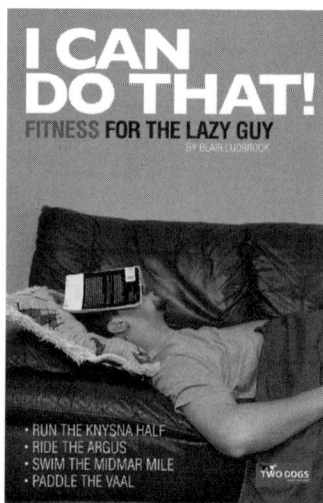